SENATOR WILLIAM EZRA JENNER
OF INDIANA

Remembered by his son

William Edward Jenner

Copyright © 2014 William Edward Jenner

ISBN: 978-0-9912095-7-6

All photos are from the personal collection of the author.

Hawthorne Publishing
15601 Oak Road
Carmel, Indiana 46033
www.hawthornepub.com
317-867-5183

DEDICATION

TO THE SENATOR'S GRANDSONS AND MY SONS
SCOTT, PATRICK, ANDY AND JOE
AND THEIR CHILDREN
MAX, JENSEN, ANNIE KATE, MITCHELL, TATUM, TAYLOR,
LUCY, JACKSON, MARY GRACE, JANE, KAIYA AND HARPER

AND ESPECIALLY FOR MY WIFE, ANNE,
WHO MADE THIS DEDICATION POSSIBLE

(l to r) Patrick, Joe, Scott and Andy

TABLE OF CONTENTS

FOREWORD

Why do I feel compelled to write about my father? Perhaps as I grow older, I feel my own mortality and want to express this history and these thoughts so that my own sons and our grandchildren will have them.

A large part of my mission in writing this book is to honor the good man who was my father. My father was, beyond his national and state reputation, a loving father who always placed my welfare first and did everything he could to help me achieve my goals. I could always rely on his promises and knew that if he said that he would help me, he would do all in his power to do so. I never had to doubt his motives, intentions or love. If I have had any success as a father to four sons, it is because I tried to follow his example in my relationships with them.

A friend who had grown up with a very dysfunctional father once told me that when he had children he resolved above all else in his life to be a good father. He failed in that, however, because he later realized he really didn't know how. He had no role model. I feel blessed that I did.

My father was a generous and humorous man, and this generosity extended beyond his family and into the circle of associates he made in his professional life. He was friendly and loyal to these friends as they were, for the most part, to him. These political and personal cohorts were known as the "Jenner Gang." They stayed together, even though they didn't control a great deal of patronage, because of Dad's charisma and the fact they could always count on his word. He always told me that in politics, more than any other profession, "your word is your bond." If you lie in a contract or business deal, you can be sued. There is no legal action for breach of promise in politics.

He not only made good friends in politics, he had many good social friends, business associates and loyal secretaries. I think because he was fun to be around, essentially warm and kind, admittedly profane but never in a sexual or irreligious sense, and very warm and funny, people gravitated to him. Many of the United States senators who disagreed with him politically and on policy and legislation liked him as a person.

In his 50-year marriage to my mother, he was kind, loving and generous. The marriage worked primarily, however, because of the kind of person Janet Jenner was. She took care of me, their only child; kept a neat house; and had good meals prepared. She never sought the limelight even though she was attractive and had theatrical talent, which she left dormant throughout their marriage until my father's retirement from politics and their return to her hometown of Bedford in 1958.

My mother was a beautiful natural blond of great intelligence. After my birth, she gave up her career as a schoolteacher to work as a homemaker and mother. Although very much an asset to my dad politically because of her charm and naturalness, in those days when candidates' wives were largely relegated to the background, she was happy to stay there behind the scenes.

That was the personal side of my dad. I also want to put a stamp on the public side of his remarkable life, which was a testimony to a deep sense of character and strong associations and loyalty to his country and its ideals. Bill Jenner can be remembered for controversial but principled positions, for fiery rhetoric, and for being forthright and courageous in action in this country's legislative and political process in a way few public servants have even attempted.

In his conservative politics, Bill Jenner was fiercely patriotic, a believer in the basic values and the strict construction of the Constitution. He served in the United States Army Air Corps in England during World War II and in the United States Senate in the years immediately thereafter. He lived at a time when the United States was, without question, the most powerful nation in the world. He believed that our nation was great, and that we should serve the rest of the world as an example or beacon of freedom. He did not believe, however, that we should intrude ourselves into the politics and intrigues of other nations. He was probably an isolationist in the sense that George Washington was when he called for friendly relations with all nations—entangling alliances with none. He was one of the most colorful men in the Senate, known for his strongly presented views, but also one of the most respected.

Dad was, in my view, more of a populist in internal affairs. His background was that of the common man. He was fair to labor and was pro-civil rights. I do not remember him ever saying a derogatory thing about African Americans or any other ethnic group. His invective was saved for communists, fellow travelers, big spenders and one-worlders.

On news of his death, a college classmate and old friend of mine sent a clipping of the *New York Times* obituary and wrote that "[he] was such a vital, interesting, and kind man. I have always felt it a distinct privilege to have known him and spent time with him. Mr. Jenner was also one of the best fathers and husbands I have known … his distinguished and outstanding public career only served to add an extra dimension to his personal stature." I believe all my friends felt this way about my dad, and I hope the readers of this book will come to view him that way also.

I should say a word about the notating of reference sources in this book. One of the major threads to emerge from this research was my impression that newspapers and periodicals of the day were fascinated with my father. They seemed to seek him out because they knew he would give them a good story, full of quotable "Jennerisms" and pithy and intelligent comments. He had comrades in the press, and the press was notably different than the way it is now. Newspapers have always been partisan, but in the 1940s and '50s some sharp columnists and correspondents made an effort to report unbiased news and give information while still including as much color, political fire and life as they could in their stories. That is not to say that news reports of the day were always favorable to my father; at times they were not. These reporters on the hometown dailies detail Jenner's career; they bring it to life and they are by far the major source of his story. I've put into this story the names of both reporters and newspapers and the date of their postings. Indianapolis newspapers are called by their common names; papers in other cities retain their formal titles. I've also referred to book references this way. In this day of archived newspapers and easy access via the internet to digitized resources, this allowed me to avoid footnotes in the interest of moving this story forward. Complete material on sources utilized is listed at the end.

ACKNOWLEDGMENTS

It is with gratitude that I acknowledge the ideas, help, encouragement and major transcription and editing contribution of Robert G. Trimble, Professor Emeritus of Hanover College, who knew my father. His wife, Barbara and his mother-in-law, Mary M. Schubert, both had worked for my father during his political life. I am also indebted to Dave Tudor, whose Jenner career interviews were an invaluable resource, and to the Indiana University Center for the Study of History and Memory, which contains his interviews. I am also grateful for the input and suggestions of my good friends Ted and Marni Todd, and I thank the staff of the Hanover College archive, where my father's papers are housed.

SENATOR WILLIAM EZRA JENNER
OF INDIANA

"The real prophet of the new Republican populist conservatives ...
the prototype for Barry Goldwater [and] Ronald Reagan ..."
The American Spectator, Jenner obituary, May 1985

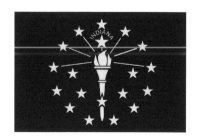

CHILDHOOD, EARLY LIFE AND EDUCATION

William Ezra Jenner never intended to be a senator. His desire was to be governor of the state of Indiana. Acceding to the wishes of his party, he ran for the Senate successfully and served as a senator espousing conservative ideals. Then, the last time the Republican Party called on him to run again with good prospects for election, he declined. He wanted to leave Washington behind, return to Indiana and live the life of a Hoosier with his wife and high-school-aged son. William Jenner was nothing if not independent minded. He followed and trusted his own inclinations.

Dad was born in Marengo, Indiana, on July 21, 1908. This little town is located in Crawford County, a rural and thinly populated area nestled among the hills of southern Indiana approximately 40 miles west of New Albany, Indiana, and Louisville, Kentucky. It is bounded on the south by the Ohio River.

At first glance Crawford County would seem a poor bet to produce a United States senator. With a population of less than 10,000, no industry to sustain a work force and farmland that is poor and in large part untillable, it ranks near the bottom among Indiana's 92 counties in size, population and economic wealth. It is a county where life has been cheap, with 20 murders from 1920 to 1984. Most of the convicted murderers were proven guilty only of manslaughter, and none ever received the death penalty.

Because of a lack of industry and productive farmland, people in Crawford County who had a job either worked in the schools (a political subdivision of county government) or for the county. As a result politics was a serious matter, and the inhabitants were very active in the practice of political warfare. Voter turnout in the county generally exceeded ninety percent. These were actively partisan people.

This was the crucible that produced William E. Jenner, who probably was Indiana's most colorful politician of the twentieth century. He was a son of Republican County Chairman, Lycargus Linwood "Woody" Jenner, who was 31 at the time of his son's birth, July 21, 1908. Bill's mother, Jane McDonald, who had been an orphan, was 30 years old. His brother Donald had been born in 1905. Loren Jenner, another brother, was born in 1913.

There are certainly a lot of William Jenners in this family to keep track of. Woody Jenner was himself the son of W. E. Jenner, who was listed in the 1895 *Indiana Gazette* as a "Dentist and Justice of the Peace." However, this "Billy Jenner" must have been part of the plan to operate a general store in Marengo, as it was always named W. E. Jenner and Sons.

Dad remembered his grandfather as saying he fought with northern General William Sheridan in the Civil War. Billy is listed in the complete roster of Crawford County Civil War soldiers as having been a private for the Indiana Independent Cavalry, a unit from his home area. The returned veteran soon showed himself as quite versatile, working as a tinsmith and stove builder. He also became a dentist who made false teeth and sold a medicine called "Jendine," a suppository for hemorrhoids. A small man who wore a bowler hat, Billy would take his wagon into the woods and gather elderberries from which he made elderberry wine, which he sold. His wife Sarah, also known as Sally, had been Sarah Waltz before she was married. The Waltzes were one of the original families of the town of Marengo. A search of Crawford County real estate records reveals a Waltz addition to the town of Marengo.

Woody, his son, was a small-town entrepreneur, building the Jenner Garage in 1917. This town landmark was a brick structure with a workshop below and storage room above. Woody sold the first automobile in the county to Willis Pierson in 1910 and as years passed had his name on a very active Ford agency. Newspapers of the time show him sponsoring the old fiddlers' contest in Marengo in 1926 at the Rialto Theatre, which he also owned. First prize was a Ford automobile and a trip to Detroit. Five hundred people attended the contest, although the Rialto had only 360 seats.

Dad remained attached to his family all his life. His father was also a dedicated family man. Woody had three siblings: an older brother Jimmy, a brother named Harry and a sister named Gertrude. Jimmy moved to Louisville and founded the very successful Jenner Engraving Company there. James and his wife had no children. Gertrude married a man named McCloud and moved with him to Mississippi. She had at least one son, whom she named Jenner McCloud. These were Dad's uncles and aunt. He did not know what became of Harry Jenner.

I asked Dad to sit down with me in 1982 or 1983, after the birth of his grandson William Joseph Jenner in 1981, so we could record some of his family and career history. He would have been 74 or 75 at the time. These memories are, then, his own, directly from him as are many of the stories in the book.

He loved most of all to speak about his dad. There was more to the history of Woody Jenner than just that he loved politics and selling and managed a Ford agency. The man had only a fourth-grade education and early in his life operated a streetcar in Louisville. During the "Cleveland Panic" of 1893, when he was 16, he worked at the Marengo stone quarry for 25 cents a day. Later he went into business with his brother Jimmy. Together they bought a hardware store in Marengo for $2,000, then soon branched into other areas such as feed and furniture. Jimmy moved to Louisville, and in 1908 Woody obtained the Ford agency. The business was named W. E. Jenner and Sons, carrying the name of his father. Billy Jenner did not die until 1915, even though son Woody actually ran the business. Henry Ford had incorporated the Ford Motor Company in 1903, but by the 1920s the car company was selling tens of thousands of cars. The Model T was a national phenomenon, so Woody and the others in the family were involved in something successful. Dad grew up in the auto business.

As a 12-year-old boy in 1920, Dad remembered taking the Southern Railroad train that ran through Marengo to the Ford plant in Louisville, paying for a vehicle there with a cashier's check and driving the vehicle over primitive routes to Marengo for resale. Because of the miserable condition of the roads, the vehicle would suffer numerous blowouts or flat tires on the trip from Louisville. They had to be repaired by Dad, whose feet could barely reach the pedals of the car. Car travel in those days was an ordeal. Often the vehicles would get stuck in the mud and have to be pulled out by a team of horses. Once the car was delivered and sold, Woody or my dad would have to take the new owner out and teach him to drive it.

Dad remembered his mother as a churchgoer (Methodist), a good mother and housewife and most of all a wonderful cook. She had been orphaned at a young age, and she and her siblings had been "farmed out" to different families. She finally settled in Marengo and was raised by a distant relative, "Uncle" Bill Gregory. Dad felt that because of her lack of loving parents, she had difficulty expressing affection, but she did show her love through cooking. His father was more affectionate than his mother, but his mother was always there when he got home from school.

His first home, he recalled, was built from yellow poplar that his dad had purchased from the then-defunct Marengo Academy. After the death of William E. Jenner, Billy, in 1915, his son Woody with his family moved to a larger brick home to take care of Woody's mother Sally. Sally died in 1920.

Dad attended an all-grade school in Marengo. One of the teachers, whom they called Aunt Mary, would conduct surprise fire drills on a regular basis. She would stand inside the school until all the children had exited in orderly fashion. Dad wondered what would happen if one day there was a real fire, and, to find out, he managed to set off a fire alarm. Aunt Mary panicked, thinking there was a real fire, and bolted from the school ahead of the children. Dad was found out and received an expulsion for several days.

He remembered as a child performing as an actor and singer in the Marengo Cave, a regional attraction that was pitch-black inside but illuminated by carbon lights. He received $1.50 for each 10-hour day.

The main sport in Marengo was basketball. The team had no uniforms, shoes or a gymnasium and played in their stocking feet on ground that often was muddy. Their thrill each year was boarding the Southern Railroad for Tell City and the sectional tournament. The team would always lose but loved the train ride and staying overnight in a hotel.

World War I did not seem to have much effect on Marengo, but the 1918 influenza epidemic did. This plague swept the world and killed an estimated 50 million people. (World War I claimed an estimated 16 million lives.) There were 675,000 deaths in the United States, and mortality rates were highest among young adults. Approximately 25 percent of the U.S. population was affected.

Dad remembered that his oldest brother, Donald, was badly afflicted and almost died. The only medicines known at the time were aspirin and whiskey, and because Indiana was a dry state, that remedy was not easy to find. Dad recalled his father and Henry Waynick driving to Louisville with him (then a 10-year-old) to buy a Model T touring car–load of whiskey. Dad was told to lie atop the boxes that were covered with a blanket and to act very sick. This would not have been very difficult, for at that time Dad was a small and somewhat sickly child. When they crossed the K and I bridge from Louisville into Indiana, they were stopped by the Indiana police. Grandpa Woody told the police that they were welcome to search the vehicle, but his son was gravely ill and he had just picked him up from the Norton Infirmary. The police, seeing the obviously ill child, declined to search the vehicle, and the whiskey made its way back to Marengo. Apparently Dad had been a very convincing actor.

During most of Dad's childhood, Marengo had no electricity. He remembered standing and holding his father's hand when the lights were first turned on in town. I am impressed at the breadth of what occurred during his lifetime—electricity, indoor heat and air conditioning, automobiles, air flight, television and finally a man on the moon, as well as the Great Depression and two world wars. How little our generation has seen in comparison: a little technological innovation and the computer.

Dad's first real taste of politics came in 1925. An article dated April 2, 1925, announced that William E. Jenner, a junior in Marengo High School, had been selected to represent Crawford County in the junior legislature of Indiana. The Junior Assembly was sponsored by the state Department of Education and was made up of representatives from high schools around Indiana. More than 100 boys and girls were seated when the two houses of this junior state legislature convened in Indianapolis.

Dad was elected president pro-tempore of the senate, having defeated the Democrat for the office by a vote of 29 to 18. The assembly passed legislation calling for the teaching of athletics in high schools, religious training in state universities, the teaching of the U.S. Constitution in all schools and the establishment of a school for the blind. The appropriation bill called for $100,000, but an amendment Dad proposed reduced the amount to $5,000.

The most heated debate was over a child labor amendment. Dad's speech against the amendment won him distinction at the assembly, and the amendment was defeated in both houses by a narrow margin. He made speeches opening and closing the session.

On his return to Marengo he addressed the high school about his experiences and was accorded an ovation. Preceded by the school's concert band, he was carried on the shoulders of fellow students through the streets where citizens lined the sidewalks.

This was the 17-year-old's first experience in politics, and he liked it. The success of being elected to the highest position in the Junior Assembly would certainly be a heady experience for a young boy from the small town of Marengo.

By 1925 he had completed most of his high school credits. That summer his father drove him to Danville, Indiana, and enrolled him in Central Normal College, where he finished the final requirements. At convocations held at the college that summer, he and the other students were kept abreast of the progress of the Scopes Monkey Trial in Tennessee.

That same summer a new opportunity beckoned for Bill Jenner. A woman from Marengo named Maggie, who was a nurse and had attended the sick child of a wealthy New York family, called Dad's mother. She advised my grandmother that the Lake Placid Club School, an exclusive preparatory school in Lake Placid, New York, had contacted her employer. Apparently the school was looking to "diversify" and was offering scholarships to a few poor boys from other parts of the country. Because she had been close to the wealthy family, they called her to ask if she knew anyone in the Marengo area who might qualify for a scholarship. She advised Jane, his mother, that she wanted to nominate young Bill Jenner.

My grandfather and grandmother discussed the matter, and because they felt he was still too young for college at 17, they thought this preparatory school being offered to the family would present an appropriate opportunity.

In the fall of 1925 Dad's father put him on the train bound for Lake Placid, New York. Dad said he had never felt homesickness before, and it was awful. He even phoned his father and begged to come home. His father, however, said that if he came home it would be a sign that he didn't have "guts enough." Woody told him to stay.

Dad did stay, and he thrived. He had been small, but because of the regularity of the schedule and required participation in football, ice hockey and basketball, he rapidly filled out to his adult size of 5′ 11″ and 185 pounds. He even won the highest award of the school in 1926—the School Seal Prize for scholarship and athletic ability. Dad got to travel to New York City and see the 1926 World's Fair in Philadelphia. All in all, he believed his experience in the East was a very broadening experience.

Ira A. Flinner was the supervising director of the school at the time. Flinner later served as the headmaster of the school, which eventually was named and still exists as Northwood School. The headmaster in 1925–26 was Robert W. Boyden. Dad was clearly a midwestern exception amidst many New Yorkers and others from the coast. The makeup of the school was definitely eastern. In Dad's class of 35, 19 were from New York and 10 from other eastern and New England states. There was one student from Paris, France; one from Alabama; one from Wisconsin; and one from Florida. And then there was the one from Marengo, Indiana.

At the time of his graduation from Lake Placid, Dad was called in to the office of Headmaster Boyden and asked which college he planned to attend. At that time the principal schools that were recognized as tops by the eastern preparatory schools were Dartmouth, Harvard and Yale. When asked what school he wished to attend for his college education, he said Indiana University. Professor Boyden said he had never heard of it. He got down a book and exclaimed, "Jenner, they let girls go to school there!" whereupon Dad said, "That's why the HELL I want to go there."

Politics was in Dad's family tree, at least the recent part of it. His father was elected Republican county chairman in 1928, after Dad had returned from the East. Dad always said that you inherit your religion and your politics. He did, becoming a Methodist and a Republican.

Dad attended Indiana University at Bloomington in 1927, a school of less than 2,000 students at the time. Lee Waynick from Marengo saw that Dad pledged Delta Tau Delta fraternity. Red Woolery from Heltonville was also a Delt who became his best friend, later serving as best man in his wedding. Harold Handley, later to become governor, was also a member of the same fraternity, as was at a later date Frederick Landis, Jr., who would serve on the Indiana Supreme Court. He was a nephew of baseball commissioner Kenesaw Mountain Landis.

Hoagy Carmichael was also attending IU at the time and was generally known for playing the trumpet, Dad said. However, on occasion, Carmichael would pound out songs on the piano at a popular soda shop called the Book Nook. Branch McCracken, later to coach IU to the 1953 national basketball championship, was playing on the IU basketball team, developing the pivoting style which made him one of the best players in IU's history.

Dad was elected president of his fraternity and was named to the honorary Sphinx Club. He also developed some negotiating skills while at IU. He did not care for ROTC and stopped attending class. Colonel Robinson, the ROTC leader, advised him that he would not be able to graduate because he had not completed ROTC. Dad discovered that Robinson's son, also a member of Delta Tau Delta, had gotten drunk one weekend, so with this knowledge Dad went to the colonel and said he would not report his son to campus officials if Robinson could get his ROTC record "straightened out." Robinson was able to clear up Dad's ROTC record so he had the necessary requirements for graduation.

Dad enjoyed performing in the college chorus, where he sang and danced. "I would liked to have had a career on the stage. I was a pretty good singer in those days," he said.

He met his future wife, Janet Cuthill, in his sophomore year, 1927. She had transferred from Northwestern University and was trying out for Garrick Club, a dramatic group of which he was already a member. After the tryouts they took a bus to Brown County for an initiation dinner. He aggravated her at the dinner by tearing up her table decoration. At some point in the evening she had to perform for the qualification. After she performed, he came to her and said, "I'm sorry. I voted for you but you didn't make it." She learned, however, that she had been voted a member. She considered Dad a "real pain in the neck" when they first knew each other.

Janet had known Dad's friend Woolery at Bedford and had dated Clarence "Oonie" Donovan from that same town. Donovan was captain of the Notre Dame basketball team and president of the sophomore class. He invited Janet to Notre Dame, where he and she led the sophomore cotillion in 1927. Later Donovan, a Bedford attorney, a Democrat and a Catholic, and his wife became close friends of my parents.

Dad was attracted to Janet, but he wanted to be a "big man on campus" and date around. He felt that this enhanced his chances of being elected to the Sphinx Club. However, he did not want Janet to date, and this led to conflicts.

She did finally introduce him to her parents, Billy and Janet Cuthill. They were not impressed; the most complimentary thing they could muster was that "Bill has nice eyes." In any event, Janet and Bill were married on June 30, 1933. Red Woolery was best man and Kathryn Quinn from Bedford was the maid of honor. It was so hot in the church that day that the candles melted.

Janet had graduated from IU in 1931 at the height of the Depression. Woody was on the school board and got her a job teaching in Marengo for $500 a year. She lived with the Waynick family while Dad was completing law school.

Before he could marry, however, Dad had had to get a profession, to prove that he could support a wife. He entered Indiana University law school in 1931. There were only 68 students in the school and two of them were black. Paul McNutt was the dean of IU Law School. The students somewhat scornfully noted that he could only teach by reading from notes. McNutt would become a political foe of Dad's. When Dad entered politics, he referred to McNutt as "the soldier who never fired a gun, the lawyer who never tried a case, and the dean who never taught a class." McNutt, a Democrat who opposed the nomination of FDR in 1932 and was never liked by Roosevelt, who called him "that blond SOB from Indiana," became governor of the state. Later Roosevelt appointed McNutt as ambassador to the Philippines and quipped to an aide, "I think that's far enough to send him."

Dad did not particularly enjoy the study of law. It was, to him, "something you had to do to get there." He graduated from the IU law school in 1932 with an AB and an LLB degree. Driving a Model A Ford on a job search to Louisville and Indianapolis, he found he could not get an employment offer. He volunteered to work for free, but it was the height of the Depression, and no law firm could use him.

Dad finally decided to open his own law practice in nearby Paoli. He was able to rent two rooms for $10 a month. Woody asked if he got a job. He said, "I am going to open my own office." Woody asked, "What will it take?" Dad said he needed a cot, a desk and three chairs, and a set of statutes. He reckoned he would need about $200. Woody would not give him the money, telling Dad to borrow it at the bank. He wouldn't sign a $200 note, either. Woody was wary of co-signing a note because he had done so previously, and after the borrower defaulted, Woody had to pay off the note.

Dad's first case was a jury trial involving one Bessie Hancock, who was accused of bootlegging. He charged her a fee of $75 for a four-day jury trial. His defense was that the sheriff had planted the illegal alcohol in her house—entrapment. The jury hung. The prosecutor decided to retry her. This time she could only pay a retainer of $15. The prosecutor offered a deal of no fine and a six-month sentence—all suspended in return for a plea of guilty. Bessie reluctantly agreed to the deal.

However, Dad discovered that the plea bargain had to be approved by the governor, Paul V. McNutt. The young lawyer had to travel to the statehouse in Indianapolis to seek the approval of the former law school dean whom he had criticized in political speeches. Luckily one of the classmates from his law school was working for the governor and got him in to see McNutt. McNutt not only approved the plea agreement but was so nice that it made Dad "feel like a heel."

Jim Tucker, who lived in neighboring Orange County and had attended law school with Dad and later was elected Indiana secretary of state, affirmed that Bill Jenner had the same personality and approach to life and politics his entire life. In an interview by David Tudor in May 1971, recorded for what became the Jenner Indiana University series, Tucker said, "Bill never changed. He's the same Bill Jenner who practiced law here [Orange County] in 1934. Marengo people called him Tootie. The senate never went to his head. Marengo never washed off Bill. He wouldn't let it."

Tucker also recalled that Bill cursed a blue streak: "His whole family did that, not just Bill. His dad and his brother Donnie, you would hear them talking and you couldn't tell which was which because their voices were the same and [they would] just swear like troopers."

Dad practiced law in Orange County in 1933 and 1934 and was elected state senator from Orange County in 1934. He worked as co-counsel with locally famous criminal attorney Charles T. "Pekey" Brown in 1933, and they won a murder acquittal for Donald Willis, who was charged with killing William Archibald in his home. The jury trial lasted four days, and the jury deliberated less than an hour before returning a verdict of "not guilty."

The story is told that one day during the Depression Bill Jenner, Jim Tucker, George Prime and Sherman Minton from New Albany were all involved in the Orange County Courthouse in a case that concerned only a few hundred dollars. Tucker was to become secretary of state, Jenner a U.S. senator, Prime an Indiana appellate court judge and Minton a U.S. senator and U.S. Supreme Court justice.

However, Dad found making a living in Paoli and Orange County a bit difficult. At that time the area contained a large Quaker population. They called each other "Brother" and "Sister" and did not seem to be very litigious, willing to settle disputes in their own way.

Dad of course by 1933 had a wife to support. After the wedding they lived in Marengo with Dad's parents while he practiced law in neighboring Paoli. They were anxious to have their own home, so in 1935 they moved to adjacent Martin County. Judge Frank E. Gilkinson had been elected Martin circuit court judge in the 1934 election, and his office was available for rent. Dad said moving to Shoals proved to be a wise economic move. Unhindered by religious restraint, people in the rough-and-ready river town of Shoals, Indiana, would say, "I don't care what it costs. I want to see that SOB in court."

Dad was making good money, and they soon built a lovely home overlooking U.S. Highway 50. It still stands today across from Marshall Motors on the north side of the highway and is the last home east of "Jug Rock" located in the adjacent woods. The home cost, including labor and materials, was $1,700. Dad's office consisted of two small rooms over Bun Stiles's grocery store in downtown Shoals. The rent was $6 a month.

Lawyer Jenner won another defense verdict in a murder case in Shoals. He made a legal plea of self-defense (although witnesses said the victim was driving a team of horses at the time). His principal argument was that the victim was a rotten character who "needed killing." The jury must have agreed, returning a "not guilty" verdict in a matter of minutes.

It was during his time in Shoals that Dad made the acquaintance of Hugh Gray, who was to become his lifelong friend. Hugh was a lover of nature who had attended Indiana University and lettered in track. He was strong and wiry, with a wry sense of humor. Hugh was Dad's adviser in picking juries, and later as 7th District Republican chairman, was his eyes and ears in Indiana when Dad served in the Senate in Washington, DC.

In 1937 he and Dad purchased land and built a cabin together on the White River, which has remained in the family ever since. (Hugh and his wife Eva had no children and deeded their interest in the cabin to me on their deaths.) Hugh bought the logs for $25 from an old general store and post office in a small Hoosier town called Oak Ridge. He let Dad in for $12.50. When the cabin was built they had a total of $500 in it. They used it as a retreat and often had political strategy sessions there. Senator Capehart and Governors Gates and Handley came to this rural retreat.

At the cabin they needed to drill a well to get drinking water. They hired a one-armed man with a homemade drilling outfit mounted on an old Model T chassis to drill the well. According to Hugh, the man drilled down 67 feet and hit water, so they told him to drill 10 more feet for a pocket. They were standing there and the man said, "You know, we could drill down just a little further and we'd have oil." Dad said, "Stop that goddamn rig. We don't want oil; we want water."

Dad came to Hugh one day in the 1940s and told him that his mentor, Harry Fenton, was dying. Fenton was the only paid member of the Republican Central Committee in the 1930s and served as secretary of the party. Harry wanted some squirrels before he died. Hugh nodded. "We'll get Harry some." The next morning Dad and Hugh went hunting and were having no luck. It was dry, and they were making noise in the woods. Hugh said, "Now, Bill, I'll pull my boots off, and you take them and go to the other edge of this woods and wait for me. I'll go barefooted and kill some squirrels." A little while later Dad was sitting on a log, smoking a cigarette. He looked up and there was Hugh with four squirrels for Fenton. Friendships and politics went hand in hand in southern Indiana in those days and it was hard to tell when one let up and the other began.

II

INDIANA STATE SENATE

Although Dad could have made a good living as an attorney, he had been bitten by the political bug. He ran for the Indiana senate and was first elected in 1934. On September 21, 1936, the *Indianapolis News* carried a story that Jenner of Paoli, age 28, the youngest member of the Indiana senate, keynoted the Republican state convention in June 1936 and also had been selected as an assistant to Fred Purnell of the speakers bureau of the Republican national committee. In 1937 the 12 Republican members of the 50-man Indiana senate selected Jenner as their minority floor leader, "regarding him as their best orator...."

However, Dad's legislative career did not start on such a positive note. The election process had shown him capable and worthy of notice. He had been elected from Lawrence County, my mother's home area. Her own mother was a beautician, and her father and several uncles worked in the local stone quarries. He had conducted a vigorous door-to-door campaign and was elected to the senate seat in November 1934 at the age of 26. He would become the youngest party floor leader in the history of the state.

Here was the problem: the 1934 election had followed the 1932 Roosevelt landslide. There were only 12 Republican senators. Dad said, "Hell, we could have held our caucus in a phone booth." Paul V. McNutt, who had been elected governor in 1932, had imposed a kind of Indiana New Deal. In 1933 he centralized state government, reducing state departments from 169 to eight, and pushed through legislation that centralized most expenditures and patronage in the hands of the governor, as William B. Pickett has shown in his book *Capehart: A Senator's Life, 1897–1979*.

According to Irving Leibowitz's book *My Indiana*, which summarized major stories during his time on the *Indianapolis Times*, Dad sought advice from Harry Fenton on how to act in the legislature. Fenton told him to "set your ass down and don't say a damn word for thirty days." Dad followed the advice so well that he dozed off at one session and fell out of his chair. The presiding officer, Lieutenant Governor M. Clifford Townsend, was quoted in the *Indiana Sentinel* as saying at a statewide meeting of women at the Athletic Club in Indianapolis, "I can't tell you a thing about Jenner. He's been asleep for thirty days." When Dad went home for the weekend he was teased about the quote. He was furious and met with Harry Fenton at Republican headquarters on Monday. He yelled at Harry, "That's what I get for listening to you." Fenton told him to "calm down and when a good opportunity presents itself, take the floor and let'er rip."

As the *Star* reported on February 1, 1935, the opportunity arose fairly quickly. Jacob Weiss, the Democrat majority leader, wasn't content to have one of his bills pass. He waved it before the gallery and boasted, "This is just another promise of the Democrat platform being fulfilled." Jenner was on his feet and was recognized by the surprised Lieutenant Governor Townsend. His rage poured out as he lambasted the Democrats for what they promised and what they actually delivered. Arms waving, the young senator strode across the floor toward Senator Weiss and roared, "Didn't you Democrats promise to give jobs to the 15,000,000 unemployed, hungry and hopeless people in this nation?" Jenner continued, "You said a moment before that the Democratic Party regards its platform pledges sacred." "And isn't it a fact," Jenner went on, shaking his fist for emphasis, "that not one of the Democratic platform promises has been carried out?"

Jenner led the minority attack on additional spending in the state budget. He forced the majority to admit "the budget was $5,000,000 greater than the 1933 budget bill." Jenner asked, "Why the increase in times like these?" The budget was $50,399,042.

During the session, Indiana became the 24th state to ratify the proposed Child Labor Amendment to the Constitution. All the Republicans voted against the amendment and named Jenner, the youngest, as their spokesman. Republican opposition centered on the fact that the amendment prohibited anyone under the age of 18 from working.

Jenner spoke, "Let's not act as politicians. Let's act as men ... No person on the floor would vote for child labor," Jenner declared. "But this is not a child labor amendment. It does not refer to sweat shops, nor long hours, nor even to children." He declared that many persons between 16 and 18 were married or were heads of households by force of circumstances resulting from death of parents. Many worked their way through school. "What are we to do with them? Shall we make them loafers?" Jenner pointed out that the state of Indiana already had in its statutes good child labor legislation.

Jenner, having started this way in the halls of power, continued throughout the session to lambast, complete with facts and figures, the majority. Weiss led passage of a new liquor control bill in the session, a bill opposed by the Republicans and some Democrats as a "private profits grab." The vote was 32 to 19 in favor. During the debate Jenner charged, "Senator Weiss is the agent for a Gary liquor concern, and you can prove it by going down to the Secretary of State's office and looking it up." In fact, incorporation papers had been filed on March 8, 1935, for the Royal Wine and Liquor Corporation of Gary, Indiana. Senator Weiss was the resident agent, and his brother, Ezra Weiss, was one of the incorporators and a member of the board of directors of the corporation (*Times*, March 9, 1935).

In 1936 Jenner was busy making speeches against the administration of McNutt, his former law school professor. In a speech in Shelbyville he accused the "flaxen haired beauty from Bloomington" of giving too much power to the national government over unemployment, old-age pensions and health in order to make peace with FDR, in hopes that McNutt could have a place in the President's cabinet, if Roosevelt was re-elected. Jenner charged, "He even visited the White House and spent a night there recently, and he slept in the bed of Abraham Lincoln. Thank God Lincoln couldn't know it!" (*Shelbyville Republican*, March 13).

In 1937 Jenner returned to the Indiana senate as minority floor leader. He announced "that it will be the purpose of the Republican senators to offer constructive criticism on all legislation of an important nature." He asserted that the minority "would be helpful in the enactment of beneficial measures, and it may be expected … to oppose any and all bills offered in the interest of special groups, bills that are dangerous … or measures that fail in their purpose to accomplish anything but the cluttering up of the statutes."

He charged "racketeering" under present Indiana alcoholic beverage laws and introduced a resolution to create a 12-member bipartisan committee to study liquor laws of other states and recommend changes to existing legislation. He charged that liquor prices were as much as $1 a fifth higher in Indiana than in neighboring states (*News*, January 8, 1937).

Jenner attacked newly elected Governor Townsend, charging that the governor had the 1921 nepotism bill repealed so that he could give a $3,000 a year job to his son, Max Townsend (*Bloomington Daily Telephone*, June 26). He also charged that Townsend had exceeded the 1935 $50,000,000 budget of Governor McNutt with an $89,000,000 budget in 1937, to finance a network of state bureaus and commissions that had outgrown the statehouse and another 6-story building. He asserted his belief that citizens can solve local problems at home "without having to go to the dome of the capitol in Indianapolis." Jenner blasted the two percent club "which exacts tributes from state employees without making public any statement of receipts or disbursements." McNutt, who had served as governor from 1932 until 1936, had built a large bureaucracy in the state government, centralizing power in the governor's office. Much of his success had come from the two percent clubs that required state and local elected and appointed officials to pay 2 percent of their earnings as a political contribution.

Jenner vowed that the Republican Party would return to power "when the public tires of waste, dictatorial government, unsound money, unbalanced budgets … and centralization of power."

In the 1937 session Jenner demonstrated that he was not controlled by big business and that he could play politics in a rough and tumble way. The railroad unions were pressing for the passage of a full crew law that would require a full crew on trains at all times. Their justification was based on safety. The railroads, however, regarded the measure as featherbedding, finding ways to unnecessarily pad out their ranks and incomes, and lobbied strongly against passage of the bill. Dad, after having been lobbied, asked Harry Fenton, secretary of the state Republican Party, how much money the railroads had contributed to the last Republican campaign. When Fenton advised him that they had not contributed, he and Fenton knew the reason. The 1932 Roosevelt landslide had devastated the party. They were a distinct minority with only 12 of 50 senators in Indiana. The railroads were concentrating on the Democrats. Actually, the full crew bill had been defeated in previous legislative sessions with the votes of many Democrats. The railroads felt that they could forget their old Republican colleagues. Dad said, "Harry, we've got to teach these guys a lesson. We've got to show them they can't forget their friends just because we're down. I'm going to get that full crew bill passed so they'll know not to forget their friends." Dad caucused with the other Republicans at the Columbia Club, but only one senator, Walter Beardsley, agreed to stand with Dad.

The railroads got the word and put intense pressure on Jenner and Beardsley. They even had the state's national committee man, George Ball of the Ball Brothers company in Muncie, call Woody and say, "Your boy is about to end a very short political career with his vote on this full crew bill."

When the roll call came, the aye votes of Jenner and Beardsley were decisive, and the legislation barely passed. Dad said the railroads learned their lesson, and he was able to work with them in the future on legislation, but he "sure cost those fucking railroads millions of dollars," as he told David Tudor in his interview on the railroad incident.

Dad was by no means anti-labor. The Indiana State Federation of Labor noted that between 1935 and 1939, he voted in favor of legislation favorable to labor 26 times and in opposition only 12 times.

In 1938 Jenner announced his candidacy for re-election to the Indiana senate for Orange, Martin and Lawrence Counties. A special session of the senate was called in the summer of 1938. Again Jenner served as minority leader, generally again serving as a pain to the majority. The *Star* reported on July 29, 1938, that he called Governor M. Clifford Townsend "the Mexican jumping bean governor" because "he changed his mind so fast and so often that even the majority couldn't keep up with him." He castigated Indiana's United States Senator Sherman Minton for introducing a "gag" law in Congress to "curb and control newspapers" so that they might print only news "approved by the federal administration in power." Jenner proposed a resolution in the state senate that copies of the provisions of the state and federal constitutions guaranteeing freedom of the press be sent to Senator Minton. The Democrat majority tabled the resolution. As one newspaper wag put it, "Next to [radio star] Fanny Brice's Baby Snooks, few can ask more irritating questions than William E. Jenner, Republican floor leader."

Jenner was one of the featured speakers at the cornfield conference held on Homer Capehart's farm in Washington, Indiana, in August 1938. His speeches at this time criticized Governor Townsend as well as former Governor McNutt, attacking centralization of government that he was certain had been carried to excess under the New Deal both in Washington, DC, and in Indianapolis. He would challenge McNutt's boast that he "eliminated 2,500 state employees his first day in office." Jenner said, "That was true. He fired 2,500 Republicans. McNutt didn't add that he hired 3,500 New Dealers to replace them the next day."

The Democrat Party in Indiana by 1938 was in considerable turmoil. McNutt had his eyes on the Democratic presidential or vice-presidential nomination in 1940. U.S. Democratic Senator Frederick Van Nuys had split with FDR on Roosevelt's 1937 proposal to pack the U.S. Supreme Court. In retribution McNutt had wanted to purge Van Nuys but decided against it in the interest of "party harmony." Van Nuys was re-elected in 1938 by less than 5,000 votes over Raymond Willis. Republicans won the secretary of state's office for Jim Tucker and seven of 12 congressional seats. They gained control of the Indiana house by a 51 to 49 margin, but the state senate remained Democratic. Dad was re-elected to his second term in the state senate.

The 1939 legislative session opened in January with Jenner as Republican minority floor leader. He moved at once for a resolution to investigate election fraud in Marion County. Jenner's resolution, defeated by the Democrat majority, asserted that "a collection of politicians known as the Statehouse gang used unlawful ... methods to control the results of the election in Marion County by coercing ... thousands of public employees and relief workers to vote for a printed list of candidates representing the choice of the so-called Statehouse gang" (*News*, January 6, 1939). As the local media had it, Jenner would continue to be a thorn in the side of the Democrats for some time to come.

III

1940 GUBERNATORIAL RACE

Shortly after the 1939 session began, reports surfaced that there was a movement for Jenner for governor in 1940. He was very active that year, speaking all over the state. His supporters claimed that he was "one of the most colorful GOP leaders in many years" and that he "would make an oratorical appeal to Hoosier voters unequaled ... since the campaigns of Albert J. Beveridge" (*Elkhart Truth,* April 8, 1939). In June, State Chairman Arch Bobbitt, a prospective candidate, declared that he was "definitely out of the race for governor," leaving Kokomo attorney Glenn R. Hillis, Judge James A. Emmert of Shelbyville, and Jenner as the leading Republican candidates. It was thought that Ralph Gates would likely back Hillis, the *Star* opined in Maurice Early's April 8 column "The Day in Indiana."

On November 30, 1939, Jenner made it official by formally announcing his candidacy for the 1940 Republican nomination for governor. His slogan was "Drive out the Statehouse gang," the *News* said. Jenner's speeches generally attacked the administrations of both Governor McNutt and Governor Townsend. In a speech in Richmond he attacked "New Deal dictator rule." As a result he said state boards and commissions had increased, mental patients had been beaten and anti-nepotism laws had been repealed so that Governor Townsend could appoint his son to a high-salaried state job. Liquor laws, he contended, were established to make "New Deal favorites" rich. He charged that McNutt's 1933 governmental reorganization act was written at the Indianapolis Athletic Club, not by legislators, but by Frank McHale, Democrat National Committeeman (*Cincinnati Enquirer,* December 1). He declared that this 200-page legislative bill was introduced and made law in less than a week. He also charged that the liquor control acts were written at that same Athletic Club by a gang of unelected New

Dealers who benefitted financially from its enactment. The December 1 *Star* and all the other newspapers were having a field day. Jenner was the perfect subject for newspaper reporters to admire for spunk and guts and, sometimes, to lambast.

In his campaign, Jenner pointed out the increase in the cost of state government under the McNutt and Townsend administrations, from $37,000,000 in 1931–32 to $69,916,907 in fiscal year 1938–39 (*Star*, January 3, 1940). He attacked the two percent club as "money collected from you for their salaries, which is spent to perpetuate themselves in office." He pledged that when Republicans drove out "the statehouse gang," there would be no Frank McHales, and officers of the state would administer the government (*Star*, March 15, 1940).

Jenner, surprisingly, finished second in a field of six candidates to Glen Hillis at the 1940 Republican state convention. Hugh Gray and Jenner thought they had a deal with Emmert. Whoever received the fewest votes between them on the first ballot would move his support to the other on the second ballot. On the first ballot Hillis had over 800, Jenner about 700 and Emmert 600. Emmert double-crossed them and did not withdraw, and Hillis won on the second ballot.

Jim Tucker in his interview with David Tudor wondered why Dad even wanted the highest position in the state. "I didn't see why he wanted to be governor with his temperament and as nervous as he was ... Bill was a natural for senator. He was a good speaker ... whereas just for the humdrum administration things that the governor has to do, that wouldn't have suited Bill."

Jenner campaigned vigorously for the ticket in 1940, challenging his former law school professor McNutt to a debate "any time, any place" (*Louisville Times*, September 24, 1940). Despite the fact that Hillis lost the governor's race to Henry Schricker of Knox by less than 4,000 votes, the Republicans in the 1940 election carried control of the senate (31–19) for the first time since 1931 as well as the house 64–36. Jenner was selected as president pro tempore or majority leader in the senate, and Frank Millis, Jenner's campaign manager in his race for governor, was selected as the majority leader for the house of representatives. The *Star* headlined on November 15, 1940, "Jenner group now controls Indiana G.O.P."

It was noted by William Madigan on November 19 in that paper that Jenner and James M. Tucker, the secretary of state, had grown up in neighboring Marengo and Paoli, that they had attended IU at the same time, and both had engaged in verbal tilts with McNutt, then dean of IU's law school. Both had practiced law in Paoli, and Jenner had moved to nearby Shoals in 1935. It was speculated that Jenner would be a candidate for governor in 1944 and Tucker was the "logical man" for U.S. senator.

In 1941 an Indiana Supreme Court decision resulted in an attorney general opinion that the Indiana secretary of state should control employment and patronage at the state's license branches (136 in number). This gave Republicans their first patronage since Roosevelt's election in 1932 and gave Tucker the edge for the U.S. Senate seat. However, his term would end in 1942, and he could not succeed himself. In July 1941 Ralph Gates was elected Republican state chairman, replacing Arch Bobbitt. This was regarded as a defeat for the Jim Watson and Ewing (Rabb) Emison faction of the party. In addition, businessman Homer Capehart, who had hosted the Cornfield Conference, defeated Emison for 7th District chairman.

Jenner, on the advice of his mentor, Harry Fenton, had planned to establish residence in Hendricks County, ten miles from Indianapolis. Fenton advised Jenner that the future belonged to politicians "north of highway 40." On February 3, 1942, Fenton died. He was hailed as one of the most colorful and astute Republican politicians in the previous two decades. He had risen to prominence as secretary to Governor Warren T. McCray in 1922. He had served as secretary of the Republican State Central Committee and was Jenner's main backer. Jenner honored the man in his last days with the tribute of squirrels previously described.

History was intervening. The U.S. had entered World War II after the bombing of Pearl Harbor in December 1941. Jenner resigned his seat in the state senate to join the U.S. Army Air Corps. It was the beginning of an interlude that would not include politics, the first in Jenner's life for several years.

IV

THE WAR YEARS

Pearl Harbor was bombed on December 7, 1941, precipitating America's entry into World War II. I was born on February 8, 1942. On that day a newspaper article noted that William E. Jenner, Joint State Senator from Martin, Orange and Lawrence Counties, was the father of a son. He received the news at 12:40 a.m. on Sunday. The article headlined "Senator Has Son." It made no mention of Janet. (Dad's secretary, Wilma Wood, wrote in a scrapbook, "Wonder where Janet was while Bill was having his baby boy?")

My parents had been married since 1933 with no children. Dad said he was forced to volunteer for duty or people would say, "That clever Jenner—he finally knocked up Janet to get out of the war." Whether his reasons were political, patriotic or a combination of both, he volunteered for military service in 1942 at the age of 34, resigning from the Indiana senate after seven years of service in that body.

Mother told me he was not very ambitious in the army and gained weight. However, he did rise to the rank of captain in the U.S. Army Air Corps and was stationed in England. Mother saved correspondence from this period of their lives that provided information from that time. Apparently his initial training was in Miami, Florida, with graduation on Saturday, August 8, 1942. Subsequent to that, he was stationed in Ogden, Utah, where Mother and I joined him and lived until November 11, 1943.

On November 13, 1943, he was sent to Rome, New York, in anticipation of being shipped overseas. On that date he wrote, "Bad things only come from thinking—as bad thinking will make it so. So think about our home-to-be and what a wonderful guy that Billy is. See how I love both you and him—you'll never know." I am sure all married soldiers going to war expressed similar sentiments. My generation has never faced such an important and pivotal experience. Imagine going to war where the outcome and the ultimate fate of the world was pending.

A World War II Diary

On December 23, 1943, my dad wrote that he was "still on the high seas and despite the terrible voyage," he was surprised he had not become seasick. He hoped that by next Christmas we would all be together. On Christmas Day, December 25, 1943, he wrote that it was difficult to write because of restrictions, but that he was leaving the country and flying to another country the next day. He described it as "thrilling" but assured Mother that he would be all right. He hated the English weather and said, "I can see why England has owned and controlled three fourths of the world for four hundred years—you've got to be damned tough just to survive." The British people were great and he "admired them." On December 27, 1943, he wrote that life was pretty rugged: he was sleeping on a straw mattress. Still, he was glad to be there and didn't want to come home until it was over.

His letters in January 1944 expressed his love and longing for Mother and me and contained complaints about the failure of his foot locker to arrive, cold baths, the weather and Spam. His weekly ration consisted of one bar of soap, two razor blades, seven packs of cigarettes, three candy bars and one pack of gum. "I give my candy and gum to little boys about Billy's size. You can guess why." He concluded that he would not trade Indiana for the entire British Empire.

On February 8, 1944, he remembered that two

years ago they had gone to the hospital when she was to deliver what they thought would be a girl, Janet K., but got a "knot head" instead. Writing was a daily exercise for him. He could not disclose his location but advised that German planes were flying over. Wherever he was in England ("a long way from London") they would receive men "fresh off the boats, train them for nine days and send them off to battle stations." They lived in an old castle with bare floors and two bathrooms for four floors, slept on little army cots on British straw and huddled around a little fireplace like a "covey of quails," with everyone nursing a perpetual cold and his sinuses always bothering him. On February 23, 1944, he wrote Mom that he had visited her relatives in Scotland on a 48-hour pass, and that Uncle Sam, Isa and their son Fergie would like to come to America. Sammie was working in the shipyards for $20 a week and Isa was a waitress. He remarked that her grandfather was remarkable for age 84, and that her grandmother was fine. He had also visited Edinburgh and had seen Princes Street and Jenner's Department Store and had toured Holyrood Castle.

In April 1944 he was hospitalized with a sinus infection. By April 13 he was out of the hospital and feeling OK, but his eye was worrying him. He felt that the vision in his left eye was all but gone. By April 16 he was acting as assistant chief of personnel and training. He was aware of the race between Homer Capehart and Jim Tucker. He said both had been nice to him, so he didn't care who won.

On April 30, 1944, he wrote that the problem in his left eye had moved to his right eye. Apparently he was to have been promoted to major before the eye problem. His eyes must have become much worse by May 3, 1944, because he was hospitalized. He was discouraged, saying that he could no longer read or practice law, but he would "find something." He had not told Mother how bad it was, but he couldn't hide it now because his location would have told her something was wrong.

By May 7, his right eye was no worse, and despite his sight problem, he was not blind and seemed "lucky in comparison to the other boys in the hospital—luckier than the boys lying all around me."

By May 10, 1944, he was undergoing treatment and could not write, so John W. Buswell, a lieutenant colonel, wrote to tell Mom that his condition was serious but not hopeless, and that the cause of the problem was with the retina in his right eye. The officer wrote that Dad had "a brilliant mind and a true sense of justice and values." By this time he was in what he called the 91st General Hospital, where they "have the best eye doctors in England."

On May 24, 1944, Dad was sent home to America and was now at the Convalescent Center and Regional Station Hospital in Mitchell Field, New York. On June 8, 1944, he wrote that he had been operated on Tuesday at 4 p.m. to remove "embedded tonsil tags" which had apparently been the cause of his eye problems. The surgery had been delayed because he had lost so much weight: down to 160 pounds. His father had just visited him in the hospital.

Back home in Indiana, of course, politics was not standing still. Jenner was being informed by colleagues of both races and animosities.

With both Dad and Jim Tucker in the military, Homer Capehart had been active throughout the state at Lincoln Day dinners, and it was rumored that he would seek the nomination for U.S. senator, a post for which Tucker had previously been the favorite. Jenner wrote Martin County's Judge Gilkinson on October 16, 1943, advising that he had learned that Tucker had been wounded and would return home and would be a "splendid and winning candidate" for U.S. senator.

On January 15, 1944, Capehart officially announced his candidacy in Washington, Indiana. In March 1944 Tucker returned home with his medical discharge. Ivan C. Morgan, 9th District chairman, planned a homecoming political rally to kick off Tucker's campaign for the U.S. Senate. On March 28, 1944, Ralph Gates resigned his post as state chairman and simultaneously announced his candidacy for governor.

The 1944 Republican state convention was held at the fairgrounds in Indianapolis in June. The feature race was between Capehart and Tucker for the six-year senate term. Tucker felt that he had been promised the nomination by Gates and other party leaders prior to his entry into military service.

The race between Capehart and Tucker went down to the wire. During the roll call, Allen County's (Fort Wayne) entire delegation of 72 votes was cast for Capehart, and then Vanderburgh County (Evansville) cast 56 of its 58 votes for Capehart. At that point Tucker mounted the rostrum and moved that the nomination of Capehart be made unanimous. There was also a short-term Senate nomination to be filled because of the death of Senator Frederick Van Nuys. Tucker was then offered the short-term nomination, but he refused.

Dad was in an Army hospital and did not attend the convention. My mother attended the convention, and she was asked if Dad would accept the short-term Senate nomination. (If elected he would serve only 90 days.) She said that since he was interested in politics, she thought he would. Representative Noble Johnson of Terre Haute then placed Dad's name in nomination. Edward Hancock, a Rushville, Indiana, newspaper publisher who had been a candidate for the short-term nomination, withdrew, and Dad was nominated by acclamation. My mother accepted the nomination on his behalf. That night she told him of the nomination by phone at his hospital in Galesburg, Illinois. At first he could not hear her because of the static on the line, and then was quite surprised to learn that he had been nominated. Shortly thereafter he received a 15-day leave from the Mayo General Hospital of Galesburg and returned home to Mother and me (age 2 ½). We were living with my mother's parents at 1125 Sixteenth Street in Bedford.

Tucker had declined the short-term nomination because he was bitter about what he regarded as his betrayal by Gates and his opinion that he had been defeated because Capehart "had a lot more money." Tucker declared that at this point he had had a "bellyfull of politics." It has also been thought that the real cause of his defeat was a rather vulgar faux pas that he committed at a party held at the home of Joe Daniels, a prominent attorney and the Marion County Republican chairman when Tucker had been secretary of state. As a result Mrs. Daniels informed her husband that Tucker would be unacceptable as a U.S. senator, whereupon Daniels switched his support to Capehart. There may be some truth to this because, according to the *Star* of June 3, 1944, Capehart received 194 delegate votes in Marion County to Tucker's 18.

Dad and Tucker remained good friends, and Tucker supported him in 1948 when he sought the gubernatorial nomination. Tucker contended that the same forces who had opposed him in 1944 opposed Dad's bid in 1948. He said a lot of people were learning that Gates's word could not be counted on. Gates was a prototypical politician, with a deep gravely voice, large and gruff but in a friendly way. It was said that Gates "loved to fish in muddy waters."

Tucker went on to a successful career as a trial lawyer in southern Indiana and never again ran for elective office. He was the uncle of Marilyn Quayle, whose husband Dan Quayle became vice president.

On June 12, 1944, the Indiana Republican central committee officially notified Dad of his recent nomination for the short-term U.S. Senate seat.

By August, he was released from the hospital and started to actively campaign. His theme was that our fighting men had had enough of regimentation and wanted to return to a free society.

He attacked the communist forces seeking to take over the Democratic Party under the label of the New Deal. He charged that the once-great Democratic Party had surrendered itself to Orson Welles, Harry Bridges and the "Communists, fellow travelers, left wingers and crackpots who make up the New Deal."

He also assailed the national debt, contending that his 3-year-old son would inherit $2,000 as a part of this debt. "They say 'we only owe it to ourselves.' Well, some time when you are hungry and broke, try to borrow $100 from yourself."

Republicans did well in the fall. Capehart beat Henry Schricker by 25,000 votes. Gates defeated Samuel D. Jackson by more than 50,000 votes, and Jenner defeated Cornelius O'Brien by over 80,000 votes and thereby led the ticket.

Dad was administered the oath of office on November 14, 1944, by Vice-President Henry Wallace, becoming the first veteran of WWII to serve in the U.S. Senate and, at 36, its youngest member. He said it had changed a lot from when he was last in DC in 1930 as a $4-a-day elevator boy in the old House Office Building, an IU student earning some pocket money during the summer.

In his maiden and only address, he urged that the administration of veterans' affairs be decentralized from control in Washington to the local county level and introduced a measure calling for local veterans' service offices in each county in the United States, according to an article in the *Baltimore Sun* (November 17, 1944). The article went on to state that War Department "tipsters" expected great things from Jenner, who was "the first veteran of this war to get into high office." The reporter writing the article described him as "jovial and friendly. Jenner is built like a football player, only he's better looking." In the U.S. Senate he got through an amendment to eliminate from a flood control bill a dam proposed for Shoals on the east fork of White River. And so ended his short term in the halls of the United States Capitol building. More was to come.

William Jenner, Civil War veteran and merchant of Marengo, Indiana. He was the senator's grandfather.

My dad and his father Lycargus "Woody" Jenner in the 1930s.

Bill Jenner as a young state senator in the 1930s.

Lake Placid Club School

Lake Placid Club
Essex Co. N Y

Ira A Flinner
Director

Robert W Boyden
Headmaster

June 12, 1926

Mr. William Ezra Jenner

Marengo, Indiana

Dear Bill,

It is with great pleasure that I
give you this certicate that you have won the
School Seal Prize for the year 1926. This
means that you as a member of the 6th Form in
the Lake Placid Club School have shown by your
scholarship, your athletic ability, your good
conduct, and your service to the school thru
influence of character that you are worthy of
having your name inscribed on the School Seal
Trophy which hangs in the school to be seen
by all future students of the school.

Bill, keep your enthusiasms, keep
up your good work so well begun. The school
is proud of you, and I look for great things
from you in the years to come.

Your friend,

Robert W. Boyden

Jenner always tried to be out in front. It's a Hoosier political picnic with fun and games. Note the hats on the men at the fence. The year is 1941.

Jenner and his friend and Marion County political ally Jim Bradford, 1941.

Captain Jenner, U.S. Army. He served in England and there contracted an eye difficulty which was to plague him for the rest of his life.

Jenner Wins In Indiana

Named as Republican Senate Candidate; Incumbent Retires

Indianapolis, June 14.—(AP)—William E. Jenner, 37-year-old Bedford attorney, was named Republican candidate for the United States Senate by the State convention yesterday.

His election came after Raymond E. Willis, 70, Indiana's senior senator, withdrew from the race just before his name was to have been put before the convention.

Jenner defeated Rep. Charles M. La Follette of Evansville, a self-styled radical, 1994 to 105.

Willis, seeing no break in the tightly knit State organization line-up, thanked the delegates for honors given him in the past and urged harmony saying: "We must put aside all differences in November."

Willis, a conservative Republican who publishes a weekly newspaper n' Angola, has been in the Senate for one term, having been elected in 1940.

The convention climaxed a campaign high-lighted by sharp newspaper criticism of the State organization and its slate of hand-picked candidates, all of whom were swept into nomination.

The youthful candidate is an army veteran of World War II and has had wide experience in politics. He resigned from the State Republican chairmanship to make the Senate

Nominated by Republicans

WILLIAM E. JENNER of Bedford, Ind., army air forces veteran, and Mrs. Jenner, are shown after the Indiana Republican Convention nominated him for U. S. Senator following Sen. Raymond E. Willis' withdrawal from the race.

—Associated Press Wirephoto

1944 Jenner at the mic telling why he should be elected, in, appropriately, Tell City, Indiana.

Life Magazine *came to a general store in Bedford to record a typical Hoosier campaign stop. 1944*

Land for our family cabin on White River was purchased by Dad and Hugh Gray in 1937 and they built the log structure on a shoestring. Year after year the senator used it as a getaway with cronies or me and Mom.

Bill with wife and son, me. We are getting into our family Buick to go to the polls in '44. I have campaign cards in my hand.

The new senator is sworn in by Vice President Henry Wallace as the first World War II veteran in the U.S. Senate and its youngest member. 1944.

Not all of Jenner's outings were fishing for voters. He flew up with friends to Canada. (l to r) Hugh Gray, Dad, Doc Diefendorf and Lloyd Stroud of Paoli.

My teddy bear and I are being admired by adoring parents. Bedford was always home, even when we were traveling to and from Washington, DC. We tried to arrive in God's Country by the Fourth of July.

V

POST-WAR ATTITUDES

On April 25 and 26, 1945, American and Russian soldiers met along the Elbe. The two sides, knowing the end of the war was near, partied, drank, played music and danced together. The news of the meeting was heralded by the press: the forces of liberation had joined hands. Hope emanated from the conviction that the great powers of the world would work together for the good of mankind. Charles Bohlen, a high-ranking American diplomat, met with Dwight D. Eisenhower and his generals in Frankfort, Germany, on June 8, 1945. At the meeting General Lucias Clay spoke of the need to work with the Russians. He said, "to get trust, you must give trust."

This euphoria at the end of the war, however, had not infected Captain Jenner. He never bought the get-along-with-Stalin line. After his discharge in October 1944, he had given a campaign speech in Bloomington declaring that "Communism will destroy everything that has made America. It is anti-church, anti-religion, anti-homeowner, anti-farm, anti-God and anti-labor." These convictions, initiated before and during Jenner's short Senate term, would evolve as he continued his political life into the 1950s and beyond. Distrust of communism and its Soviet lords was one of the main thrusts of Jenner's career both in and out of the Senate. His position is worth examining.

By 1946, as Jenner began to consider a full term in the Senate, American attitudes towards trust with Russia were beginning to change, culminating in Winston Churchill's famous "Iron Curtain speech" in Fulton, Missouri, on March 5, 1946.

But Jenner had mistrusted Soviet intentions from the beginning, and at the close of the war he had begun to specify and act upon his convictions.

Only two treatises, unpublished, have been written on the senatorial career of Bill Jenner: "The Senatorial Career of William E. Jenner," by Michael Poder and "Senator William E. Jenner, A Study of Cold War Isolationism," by Rodney Ross. It is interesting to read these people's view of Jenner's position on communism and the Cold War from their vantage point in the 1970s. Ross branded Jenner as a "bewildered country politico." The culture and complexity of metropolitan Washington contrasted too greatly, he believed, with the new senator's unvarnished and homely beginnings. Jenner was, according to Ross, "unwilling to accept the complex and ever changing world of the cold war era." Ross thought that Jenner mistakenly believed that "the nature and traditional values of the common people, the spiritual essence of the nation ... had placed America above ... dogmas such as a materialistic and atheistic communism."

Jenner charged, Ross said, that bolshevism had brought the Soviet Union to the brink of disintegration. Persecution of the Kulaks in 1929 had brought great scarcity and hunger to the people. The Russian masses had rebelled and the Kulaks had resisted their physical elimination. Jenner viewed Franklin D. Roosevelt's recognition of Russia at that time as providing a life-saving psychological and economic lift to a "tottering" Soviet state.

The Indiana senator argued that firm pressure should be applied to compel the removal of Russian armed forces from the satellite countries. Jenner could not believe that Eisenhower in 1956 failed to support a strong Hungarian revolt. (During the revolt, the Hungarian Army and even some Soviet units defected and joined the rebel ranks, only to be suppressed by Soviet tanks and "Mongolian" soldiers.) Proof of strong resistance to the Soviets in Poland was also evident. Jenner was quoted: "The American Government not only offered no help to the Hungarian freedom fighters, it committed the unpardonable military offense of telling the enemy it did not intend to help."

Jenner was calling for free elections in the satellite countries under the auspices of the Allied Powers and the international news media as a way to alter an ominous trend. In place of "peaceful co-existence," Jenner advocated breaking off diplomatic relations with the Soviet Union. He stressed the evil and despotic character of the Russian leadership and believed that "non-recognition" of tyranny would aid the promotion of world harmony.

Fearing future, dangerous authoritarianism, Jenner had bitterly opposed the peace treaty of 1952, which conceded part of Germany's sovereignty to the Soviet Union and divided Germany into war time zones, thereby creating a communist East Germany occupied by Soviet troops.

Labeling the Kremlin as "international outlaws" and "an empire of death" in 1954, Jenner foreshadowed Ronald Reagan's delineation of the "evil empire" some 30 years later. Instead of what he viewed as dangerous and naive giveaways that would damage the future, he advocated a policy of non-recognition of tyranny to advance world peace.

Jenner's goal would be to hearten the subjugated masses behind the iron curtain, further asserting that the United States should not negotiate with the "gangsters, bandits and murderers" of Russia. Jenner believed that the entire communist bloc was on the verge of internal collapse because their inefficient economics could not satisfy the basic natural needs of their people, and that the United States should exploit this weakness to actually "roll-back the Soviet Empire" and weaken the Soviet control over its satellites.

This thinking was out of step with the doctrine of "peaceful co-existence" and must have seemed quaint to the Jenner commentators like Ross and Poder, who believed that détente and the SALT treaties were the only way to avoid a nuclear confrontation and mutually assured destruction of both the United States and the Soviet Union.

History seems to have produced a different verdict, which in many ways vindicates Jenner's strongly stated warnings. When Reagan declared Russia an evil empire during his presidency and prepared to develop a strategic defense system, Russia's strained economy collapsed and with it communist hegemony, leading to the separation from the Soviet Union and freedom of the satellite nations. Bill Jenner was eerily correct.

The conflicts over "cooperation," which often meant appeasement for the communist bloc, became a major background for the actions of Bill Jenner when he first came to Washington and later, as he would return as a full-term United States Senator.

VI

STATE CHAIRMANSHIP

After his short term in the Senate, Dad had returned to Bedford and opened a law practice.

On January 22, 1945, Governor Ralph Gates selected Dad to serve as his "legislative assistant for the session of the Indiana General Assembly." Gates announced that he had asked Jenner to come to Indianapolis and "spend as much time as possible acting for me as a liaison officer between my office and the General Assembly," adding that "[Jenner's] experience as a member of the Assembly will be invaluable," the local newspapers commented.

On February 13, 1945, Jenner was elected state chairman of the party by the Republican state committee. It was now the Republicans' turn to control state government. Jenner served as Governor Gates's go-between and was very successful in implementing the governor's program, including farm legislation.

Jenner always claimed he performed these duties because Gates pledged in return to support him for governor in 1948 when Gates's term expired. Governors in Indiana were limited to one 4-year term in office, and so the path to sitting in the large chair in the Indianapolis statehouse seemed a desirable possibility with the "deal" he and Gates had made.

Gates created a new state department, the Department of Veterans Affairs, to help 300,000 Hoosier veterans adjust to civilian life and aid them in securing jobs. Over 300 new industries were attracted to Indiana during his administration. The Indiana highway commission was reorganized and $78,000,000 was spent to improve the Indiana highway system. To attract teachers, the salary schedule was amended to provide $2,400 annual salaries for beginning teachers, and the state doubled local school support from $24,700,000 in 1943–44 to $48,800,000 in 1947–48. The Indiana council for mental health was created. All this was done while keeping a balanced budget by improving government efficiency and raising taxes on alcoholic beverages and cigarettes. Jason S. Lantzer discusses the achievements and history of the Gates administration in *Governors of Indiana*, edited by Linda Gugin and James St. Clair.

Always in the background in 1945 was the question of who would be the Republican nominee for U.S. senator in 1946. Senator Raymond Willis, a conservative and a favorite of the powerful Republican Editorial Association, was the sitting incumbent. It was well known that he would be opposed by Robert M. LaFollette, a Republican congressman, who was a liberal pro-union Republican from Evansville. Observers noted that Jenner, who had had experience during his short term in the Senate, was a strong possibility, and also that Congressman Charles Halleck was considering a run for the seat.

A meeting was held in Indianapolis, and it was decided to attempt to get young Halleck, the 2nd District congressman, to run for U.S. Senate in 1946. As state chairman, Jenner was delegated to talk him into running. It didn't work. Halleck felt very safe in the 2nd District and refused to run. Jenner advised Governor Gates that the party needed to select another candidate. Gates said, "No, we assigned you the job of getting a candidate. Since you failed, you must run for the Senate." Jenner said, "I've never had any desire to be a U.S. senator. I've had enough experience there in the short time I was in Washington. All I've ever wanted is to be governor. I intend to build my organization as state chairman, just as you did." Gates then said, "Look, we need a speaker and tough campaigner like you to lead the ticket. If you'll run, you come back in 1948, and we'll give you the governor's nomination." A promise was a promise, so, with that encouragement and reluctantly, my dad agreed to accept the nomination when it came and take to the campaign trail.

VII

1946 U.S. SENATE ELECTION

On March 22, 1946, making moves to implement the new plan, Jenner relinquished the Republican state chairmanship, and H. Clark Springer of Butler was voted unanimously to succeed him. Horace M. Coats remained as secretary to the party. The move was not unexpected, as it was assumed that Jenner would shortly thereafter announce his candidacy for the U.S. Senate, the full term, as the *Star* was predicting on March 23, 1946.

On March 27 Jenner did take the formal step of announcing as a candidate for the U.S. Senate. The incumbent Republican senator from Indiana, Raymond Willis, was surprised and shocked and returned to Indiana on a 10-day leave from the Senate when he learned that Governor Gates was taking a "hands off" position and would probably support Jenner (*Newsweek,* April 8, 1946).

Willis was a 71-year-old newspaper publisher who had served in the Senate since 1941. Shortly after Jenner's announcement, he spoke at the Indiana Republican Editorial Association midwinter meeting and said that Jenner's candidacy in no way altered his plans to campaign for re-election. Willis was relying on a tradition of parties to nominate senators who had consistently supported the party program as well as the advantage of his six years seniority. On the other hand, there was a general tradition that most senators at that time retired when they reached their seventies. Jenner was 37.

Willis had strong support from the influential Republican Editorial Association. In fact, on March 31, 1946, it passed a resolution asking the Republican organization "to refrain from any attempt to dictate the nomination...." After the meeting a Willis for Senator Press Club was founded, as the *Evansville Courier Journal* reported on March 31.

Although the 4th District Republicans in Fort Wayne endorsed Willis, the 9th District, under the leadership of Ivan C. Morgan, endorsed Jenner by acclamation. Jenner also had strong veterans' support, having been endorsed by a former national commander of the American Legion. The *Louisville Times* on March 27 opined that this was bad news for Willis because it indicated that the American Legion and other veterans groups were backing Jenner.

The convention was held at the state fairgrounds on June 13, 1946. Willis, seeing the handwriting on the wall, withdrew his candidacy before the balloting began. Then Jenner beat Robert LaFollette 1,994 to 105 (75 of LaFollette's votes came from his home county of Vanderburgh, which includes Evansville, as the *News* stated on June 13). Jenner's father Woody, a delegate from Crawford County, nominated his son to the convention.

On May 11, prior to the convention, Jenner was involved in a controversy with the *Indianapolis Star*. The newspaper had printed a story quoting LaFollette alleging that liquor distributors in Lake County had raised $25,000 for Jenner's campaign. Jenner demanded a retraction, and on July 22, 1946, the would-be senator filed a libel suit against the *Star* and its editor and publisher Eugene Pulliam, as well as LaFollette (*News*, July 22, 1946). He sued for $500,000 over these "false and defaming statements." Regardless of the questionable legal merit of such a lawsuit, it was clearly a gutsy move to sue the largest Republican newspaper in the state of Indiana in the middle of a senatorial campaign.

Jenner's Democrat opponent, M. Clifford Townsend, was a strong opponent. The 62-year-old had been elected to the state legislature in the 1920s and served four years as lieutenant governor and four years as governor of Indiana (1936–1940). He was a farmer and had served for two years during World War II as director of the War Food Administration. Townsend campaigned on two basic issues—world peace and continuation of prosperity at home. His speaking style was folksy, yet his speeches were like those of a professor.

Jenner, labeled as "shrewd, able, and aggressive," in the *Louisville Courier Journal* in October of that year, spoke out against the evils of the New Deal. In a newspaper article comparing the two candidates, Jenner was described as a remarkable orator, with the ability to play with his audience like an actor, making it laugh or turning it to more serious moods by use of stage gestures and voice inflection. It was noted that he was not unfriendly to labor and that some AFL units as well as segments of the CIO, mainly war veteran members, had pledged their support to him. In Shelbyville on November 2, 1946, Jenner called on workers to be citizens first and union members second. The *Courier Journal* reported that he argued that otherwise, the nation would be subject to forces that "subordinate the general welfare of the nation to the welfare of pressure groups." He said this encouraged what amounted to government by special interest groups. He would return to this theme throughout his career. I remember asking him why he retired from politics at the age of 50. He said that the power of pressure groups, labor, teachers and farmers had everyone asking government to "give me mine," and nobody was looking out for the general welfare of the nation. I believe that discouraged him more than anything.

In the campaign Jenner also assailed the administration that had created a national debt of $271 billion ($7,000 for each American family). He also criticized supporters of the Democratic Party such as communist Earl Browder, always reminding the audience that there were no labor unions in Russia. The defects of communism were pointed out in all of his campaigns.

Philosophically he called the New Deal to account for its claim to be the liberal party. "Except for spending, the New Deal has been anything but liberal," he said. "Liberalism means a system of government under which individual liberties are safeguarded. A true liberal is one who is willing to fight for individual freedom against encroachments by government" (*News*, September 13, 1946).

Surprisingly the *Star* apparently took the lawsuit he had filed seriously, and on March 25, 1947, Jenner's attorneys dismissed it on the condition that the *Star* would print a retraction. On March 25, 1947, the *Indianapolis Star* in a front-page editorial praised Senator William E. Jenner for "a spirit of broadminded public stewardship." The editorial went on to say that the *Star's* own investigation indicated Jenner was innocent of the charges made in the spring of 1946. The editorial added that Jenner "has made an excellent start as Indiana's junior senator" and commended his stand on domestic and foreign problems. Apparently the suit against the *Star* did not hurt him, as he defeated Townsend by 155,521 votes in the election.

The year ended unhappily for the Jenner family, as William Sterling Cuthill, Janet's beloved father and my grandfather, died on December 12, 1946, at the age of 62. He was a native of Scotland, the son of James and Marian Stirling Cuthill, born at Bo'Ness, Scotland, on October 22, 1884. He had married Janet Hamilton in Newark, New Jersey, on April 29, 1907, and moved to Bedford in the Hoosier state in 1908. He was employed as a stonecutter and a foreman of the Hoosier Cut Stone Company. He later served as an excise officer of the Indiana Alcoholic Beverage Commission until April 1945, when he retired to care for his wife who was in ill health. At the outbreak of World War I, he sought to enlist in the U.S. Army, but was unsuccessful due to army regulations regarding married men with children. He then went to Canada, where he enlisted in the Canadian army and saw overseas service with the 48th Highlanders.

Soon after my grandfather's death, on January 2, 1947, the "Jenner Special," a 7-car Pennsylvania Railroad train, left Indianapolis carrying ranking party members, including Republican State Chairman Clark Springer, to Washington, DC, for the inauguration of William E. Jenner as a full-fledged U.S. senator.

VIII

FIRST FULL TERM U.S. SENATE

Dad took his oath of office and assumed the full responsibilities of a U.S. senator. He was made a member of the labor and education committees. The labor committee moved to pass on to the full Senate the Taft-Hartley bill that authorized the issuance of 80-day court injunctions to block union strikes that would impede the national health or safety.

The bill passed the Senate and House but was vetoed in June by President Harry Truman. It was then passed over his veto by a vote of 68 to 25. This legislation was very important. It allowed the President, when he believed that a strike would endanger national health or safety, to request the attorney general of the United States to seek an injunction to block or prevent the continuation of the strike. The legislation was strongly supported by the recently elected Republican "Class of '46," which included John Bricker of Ohio, Bill Knowland of California, Carl Mundt of South Dakota and Bill Jenner.

Taft-Hartley is the main reason that the United States does not suffer from crippling national strikes as some European democracies do. Presidents have invoked the Taft-Hartley Act on 35 occasions. All but two of those attempts were successful. The Taft-Hartley Act's 80-day "cooling-off period" for disputes to be settled has succeeded in 70 percent of the cases. It may show to us all what can happen when good legislation is proposed and a spirit of bipartisan concern for the welfare of the nation predominates in the legislative and executive branches of our government. Twenty Democrats sided with the Republican majority to override the President's veto. Could this happen today?

Jenner also co-sponsored with U.S. Senator George W. "Molly" Malone an amendment to trim the administration's $597,000,000 European aid program to $400,000,000. The amendment was defeated 56 to 30.

Dad's first term also included a trip around the world on behalf of the Senate appropriations committee. The delegation left Washington for Argentina on October 19, 1949, and arrived back in Washington on December 10, a trip of 50 days covering 31,519 miles. He was accompanied by Senator Allen Ellender of Louisiana, Senator Theodore Green of Rhode Island and Senator Homer Ferguson of Michigan. The trip included stops in Paris, Madrid, Rome, Belgrade, Istanbul, Ankara, Cairo, Kuwait, Bagdad, Tehran, India, Bangkok, Saigon, Manila, Hong Kong, and Tokyo, Japan. Also part of the trip was a visit with the Pope. Jenner had lunch with General Douglas MacArthur in Japan and wrote home that he is "quite a man. Has a real American outlook." On November 9 he hunted in Iraq but wrote home to my mother and me: "But Oh! Billy. These poor little hungry children here made your heart ache."

With Dad's election to a full term in the U.S. Senate, we had moved to Washington, DC, in January of 1947. I was four years old. Because of the war, housing was scarce, and my parents rented an apartment in a downtown apartment building. I have a vague memory of the building and the smell of food coming from the various apartments.

I have been told that I did not adjust well there and cried all the time. My parents thought something was wrong with me and took me to a doctor. The doctor said, "Bill, the problem is this boy is used to a home, not an apartment. You need to buy a home."

My parents then went house hunting and purchased a home at 3601 Van Ness Street NW in Washington for $37,000. When Dad told his father of the purchase, Woody advised my father that he had lost his mind to pay so much for a house. He was right. Home construction resumed at a normal pace after the war, and when we left DC in 1957, my parents sold the house and all the furniture in it on contract for $25,000.

As years passed, I enjoyed living in Washington. Each year we would drive there from Bedford every New Year's Eve so that Dad could be there for the opening of the Senate. It was a 17-hour trip at the time. We would return to Bedford each summer. I remember that Dad was always home for the Fourth of July so that we could celebrate at the cabin in Shoals. Dad would then be home with us until the end of the year, and I would enroll in school in Indiana in the fall of each year, at least until the seventh grade.

I believe my mother preferred to stay out of the limelight and make a comfortable home for Dad and me. She seldom expressed political views and was a wonderful counterbalance for her more flamboyant partner. I can remember Dad coming home from the Senate often angry and frustrated from some political event. My mother would let him blow off steam for 15 minutes or so, offering few, if any, comments. After that my Dad would become very calm, and we would eat the dinner she had prepared and enjoy the rest of the evening watching "I Led Three Lives," "Treasury Men in Action," or the TV shows of Jerry Lester or Milton Berle.

As I grew older, the family's night out was Friday. Each Friday we would go to a neighborhood restaurant and then take in a movie. John Wayne movies were our, or at least my, favorites.

I would say that I had a very normal childhood. My mother's calm nature made that possible. One exception to the quiet life they led at home was a yearly trip they took to the Big Apple. Because my mother had been involved in drama and theater in high school and college and always enjoyed the theater, while we were in Washington she and Dad would make a yearly three-or-four day visit to New York City to take in the latest plays and musicals. They generally enjoyed life together while Dad was in the Senate.

However, the desire to become governor of Indiana had never left my dad's thought.

IX

1948 GUBERNATORIAL RACE

In 1948 "Draft Jenner" groups started organizing in January. Although Dad was serving in the U.S. Senate, the political action committees were formed to urge him to run for the Republican nomination for Indiana governor. Although he declared he was flattered, it was no secret that he did desire to be governor.

It was reported that most members of the Republican Editorial Association were against the Jenner for Governor movement. The editors were reported to be resentful of the 1946 purge of Senator Willis, that Angola editor and former U.S. senator, according to Indianapolis AP stringer John Jameson. Another AP reporter wrote on February 24 that the day before, at its midwinter meeting, the powerful association passed a resolution attacking the unannounced candidacy of Jenner for governor. Two days later Governor Gates issued a press release that was interpreted as evidence that he would fight Jenner's nomination for governor. He denounced reports of a "deal," a promise that he would back Jenner in 1948. Jenner insisted for his part that Gates had promised to support him for governor in 1948 in return for Jenner's help with the legislature in 1944 and his willingness to run for the Senate seat in 1946.

After he resigned the state chairmanship and was elected to the U.S. Senate in 1946, Jenner noticed that the mood of Gates and new state chairman Clark Springer had changed. The word was that Jenner should be satisfied with the U.S. Senate, and that he was getting "power hungry." Jenner went to the governor's office, found him at his desk, and asked if Gates still planned to follow through with their deal. Gates became preoccupied with his mail, so Jenner said, "All right, if that's what you fuckers think of your deals, that's OK with me. I'm going to campaign for governor and beat you."

On March 12, 1948, Walter E. Helmke, Fort Wayne lawyer and powerful Allen County chairman, announced his candidacy for the Republican nomination for governor and was endorsed by Governor Gates. On March 15 Gates fired the state officials who were backing Jenner. First on the list was Dr. Burrell E. Diefendorf, chairman of the Indiana Alcoholic Beverage Commission, a position he had held since March 22, 1945. Diefendorf was a supporter and hunting and fishing buddy of Jenner. Also fired was another Jenner supporter, Otto C. Wolfman, chairman of the state board of tax commissioners.

On March 23 Jenner announced his candidacy for the gubernatorial nomination, slamming Truman's policies and Washington life in general by saying, "I would rather sing 'Back Home Again in Indiana' on the banks of the Wabash than dance to the 'Missouri Waltz' on the Potomac River Shore."

Gates and the organization backed three candidates for governor—A. V. Burch of Evansville; Hobart Creighton, speaker of the Indiana house; and Walter E. Helmke of Fort Wayne.

Ninth District Chairman Ivan C. Morgan endorsed Jenner's nomination for governor. In April James Tucker of Paoli sided with Jenner against Gates, saying, "People are finding out things about the governor I could have told them about him in 1944." This was an obvious reference to Gates's failure to back Tucker against Capehart at the 1944 convention. On April 30 Senator Capehart also endorsed Jenner for governor and Congressman Charles Halleck endorsed Hobart Creighton.

The Marion County primary on May 4, 1948, pitted delegates filed by the Marion County organization that was lined up with Governor Gates against Jenner forces in the battle for the county's 221 delegates. James Bradford, former county chairman, led the Jenner contingent. Similar fights for delegates were waged in all of the primaries. A wild convention—the first to use voting machines—was anticipated. H. Dale Brown from Indianapolis, who was to become known for being one of the state's most notorious political "bosses," was a leader with Gates of the anti-Jenner factions.

A deal to sabotage Jenner was in the offing. This deal was confirmed by Claude Billings in his interview with David Tudor in 1971, available at the Indiana University Center for the Study of History and Memory. Billings was a former secretary of the Republican Editorial

Association and also secretary of the Republican state committee. The editors, he affirmed, were "anti-Jenner." The night before the convention, "Ralph Gates, H. V. Burch, Walter Helmke, Hobart Creighton and Billings were together at the Claypool Hotel. Gates engineered the idea that when the first ballot was over, there would be a recess when these candidates would meet. When they knew who the top man was, the other two would withdraw and urge their people to go for him. They shook hands on it. It was a gentleman's agreement. And they did, they held with it. After the first ballot … the three got together with Gates in the back of the platform…. Helmke and Burch went to the microphone and withdrew and urged their people to support Creighton, and on the next ballot Creighton won."

On the first ballot of the 1948 convention, Jenner had had a plurality and was only a few votes short of the majority needed for nomination. Jenner had 799 votes to 551 for Creighton, 243 for Burch and 230 for Helmke. However, convention chairman James Emmert delayed the second ballot so that Gates and the three candidates could conduct their meeting and get the deal affirmed: others withdraw, Creighton wins. The other candidates withdrew as planned, and on the second ballot Creighton received 931 votes to 885 for Jenner. Creighton was a 52-year-old native of Kosciusko County and had been a state representative since 1933. He was a World War I aviation cadet who piloted his own plane and was one of the world's largest poultry producers.

In the balloting Jenner carried Lake County 71 to 44. The other northern districts favored Creighton, while the 6th, 7th, 8th and 9th (southern Indiana) favored Jenner by a large margin. Marion County—the 11th District—was decisive, with Creighton receiving 122 votes and Jenner 98.

The story told to me by my dad was this: shenanigans that circumvented the rules were obvious. James Emmert, a non-Jenner man, had allowed Burch and Helmke to ascend to the platform and announce that they were withdrawing in favor of Creighton.

Convention Chairman Springer, for his part, had allowed Emmert to take the gavel in the first place because, he claimed, he had needed to use the restroom. Emmert was the same James Emmert who had opposed and allegedly double-crossed Jenner at the 1940 convention. Dad blamed Springer for cheating him out of the nomination by giving the gavel to Emmert, who then allowed Burch and Helmke to throw their support to Creighton. Dad's comment was that he hoped "Springer had pissed down his leg."

Emmert, surprisingly, was a member of the Indiana Supreme Court at the time of the convention. He served on the court from January 6, 1947, to January 5, 1959. At that time members of the Indiana Supreme Court were elected on a partisan basis.

Ivan Morgan, 9th District chairman, expressed the view of many delegates when he declared, "We have the hottest political property in Indiana in fifty years in Bill Jenner, and what do we do? We nominate a Goddamned chicken farmer."

In 1948 Jenner and Capehart both endorsed Creighton for governor. However, Jenner's ability to campaign was limited by the fact that he had been named by Herbert Brownell, Dewey's campaign manager, as chairman of the national Republican speaker's bureau for the Dewey for President campaign. In the last two weeks, however, he gamely delivered several speeches on Creighton's behalf. On October 27, in a speech supporting Creighton, Jenner charged that Truman had turned the New Deal into an *ordeal.* He also attacked the administration's so-called settlement of the Polish problem, which had left Poland stuck in the Soviet empire. Jenner said the administration had utterly violated its pledge to support the right of small nations to choose their own form of government.

However, Creighton, a man who bent from the neck and wore pin-striped suits, was defeated in the general election by the popular Henry Schricker. Perhaps the younger Jenner would have won, but he always said he also could have been defeated, which would have ended his political career. Dad had not resigned his seat, so he remained a United States senator.

X

THE MARSHALL SPEECH

Early in his Senate career Dad had visited Pearl Harbor. He was shocked to learn that more than 1,000 service men had been killed during the attack on December 7, 1941. He wondered how the attack could have been such a surprise that we wouldn't have had time to get any of the ships out of the harbor, or at least evacuate the ships. Back in Washington he researched the question and learned that General George Marshall had been advised of the attack that morning and had delayed alerting the commanders at Pearl Harbor of the attack. Marshall declined to send the warning through the navy's rapid transmission facilities but sent it instead by Western Union dispatch, which arrived after the attack had begun. (The full story of Marshall's actions can be found in the 1982 book *Infamy* by John Toland.)

In point of fact, the U.S. Army Pearl Harbor board's investigation found Marshall at fault for this delay. The *Chicago Tribune* and many other sources questioned Marshall's role in failing to warn of the attack. There is a great deal of well-founded historical data to indicate that Roosevelt and his advisers, including General Marshall, had hoped for an event that would cause the American people to want to enter World War II to aid Great Britain.

The issue before the Senate when Dad gave his speech in September 1950 was confirmation of Truman's appointment of Marshall as secretary of defense. Dad argued that control of the military was intended by Congress and the framers of the Constitution to be left in civilian hands and it was therefore wrong to appoint an army general as secretary of defense.

In the speech, held in my personal collection and widely reported, he outlined what he regarded as Marshall's failures. These included the failure to issue an adequate warning at Pearl Harbor; his role in lend-lease to Russia, the effect of which was to give the Soviet Union preference in the allocation of munitions in 1942 over our other allies and even U.S. armed forces; his role as an adviser to the gravely ill FDR at Yalta; his allowing Alger Hiss to act as executive secretary for the Dumbarton Oaks conference to establish the groundwork for the United Nations; his role in forcing the nationalist Chinese under Chiang Kai-Shek to take the communists into the nationalist government; and finally, his Marshall Plan, which as originally formulated by Marshall in his June 5, 1947, speech at Harvard University, would have aided communist Russia.

Dad backed up his charges with quotes from Secretary of State Henry Stimson, General John R. Deane, Cordell Hull, James Farley and Marshall himself. He cited the fact that Marshall was the only major figure of World War II who had declined to write his memoirs because "they have got to be accurate ... one mustn't omit."

In all the criticism the speech engendered, no one disputed the facts Jenner cited. He was widely criticized for his conclusions that Marshall was a "living lie" and a "front man for traitors." In truth and logically, while Marshall's actions might create the inference of such a charge, it wasn't possible to prove such allegations.

Jenner's speech could be termed an outlet for the frustrations that conservatives had felt from the inception of World War II through the post-war process where it seemed that the United States was giving communist Russia a large portion of the world. Something had to be wrong. He was not alone in his tarring of Marshall.

Mr. Republican, Robert Taft, voted against Marshall as secretary of defense on the grounds that Marshall's mistakes in China had led to the situation in Korea. Walter Trohan published a devastating piece on Marshall in the *American Mercury* in April 1951. On June 14, 1951, Senator Joseph McCarthy made a speech against Marshall that even liberal columnist Richard Rovere conceded was mostly true, but "meanly slanted." The facts in the speech had been researched by Forrest Davis, a respected speechwriter for Taft. John F. Kennedy in a speech in Salem, Massachusetts, on January 30, 1949, had stated, "At the Yalta Conference in 1945, a sick Roosevelt, with the advice of General Marshall ... gave ... the control of various strategic Chinese ports ... to the Soviet Union" (*JFK: The Man and the Myth*, Victor Lasky).

The *Chicago Tribune* editorialized on September 21, 1950, that "Jenner needn't worry" that the facts he cited "were not denied and they cannot be denied." The editorial hailed the speech and the courage of Senator Jenner in making it, knowing that he would be criticized by the "seaboard editors and radio announcers." The *Tribune* hailed the speech as one that is "likely to be read in the years to come."

Of course, the actions of Roosevelt and Marshall could also be interpreted as well-meaning attempts to live in a peaceful post-war world. In any event, Dad never took back a word of the speech. In his own words he said, "I nailed the son of a bitch but I paid a hell of a price."

Marshall was a popular figure, a war hero and much commended for his supervision of the effort to rehabilitate Europe. Dad made the Marshall speech on September 15, 1950. Homer Capehart was running for re-election that November, and he was very concerned that the speech might cost him the election. He came to Dad's office and said, "Bill, you've ruined me and our party." Dad told Homer that he was speaking in Fort Wayne that weekend. "I'll give them the speech word for word and see what reaction I get," he said. He received a rousing response from the audience in Fort Wayne, so he gave the same speech again in Logansport and received another favorable response. Dad then had 150,000 copies of the speech reprinted and mailed all over the state. Apparently Hoosiers were not as enamored with Marshall as was the national press, since Capehart was re-elected that November over Alex Campbell with a majority of 103,278 votes (55 percent). A lot of Hoosier voters were as concerned with the drift of the post-war world as Dad was. Dad also labeled Campbell as the "Ft. Wayne Cocktail Commando," stating that "While other Americans were facing German and Japanese bullets … the greatest danger Campbell faced was being hit by a habeus corpus … ." (Campbell served in the Judge Advocates Corps, or JAG, the legal section of the U.S. Army.)

XI

1952 SENATE ELECTION

People did not know if Senator Jenner would run for re-election in 1952 until his friend Herbert R. Hill received a telephone call from the senator saying, "I just received a call from the President." The surprised Hill asked, "Why would Harry Truman call you?" Jenner replied, "No, not Truman. President Hoover!" What did he say? "He said, 'Son, it is your patriotic duty to run for the U.S. Senate. Indiana needs you and America needs you'" (David Tudor's interview with Hill).

"What are you going to do?" Herb wanted to know. Jenner said, "I'm going to run." He was nominated in the state convention in 1952 and prepared to go to the July national convention in Chicago.

Jenner and State Chairman Cale Holder led the Indiana delegation to the 1952 Republican convention July 7–11 at the International Amphitheatre in Chicago. They were determined to prevent Dwight D. Eisenhower, the American leader at Normandy and one of the most respected men and former officers in the nation, from becoming the Grand Old Party's nominee. Their effort to offer Senator Robert A. Taft from Ohio, the conservatives' choice, was not a success, and Eisenhower became the standard bearer. Not surprisingly, and also as a result of Jenner's attack on Eisenhower's friend, General Marshall, it was no shock that Ike did not relish campaigning on the same ticket with Jenner when fall rolled around.

The often-reported hostility between the senator and the general, candidate for the highest office in the land, is most certainly exaggerated. Most Eisenhower biographies cite a campaign speech in Indianapolis as the basis for what they describe as strong hostility on Eisenhower's part. They report that Ike recoiled at Jenner's touch when he grabbed Eisenhower's arm and lifted it to the ovation of the crowd. This allegedly took place at the conclusion of Eisenhower's speech at Butler University on September 10, 1952. In fact, there was apparently some question after the July convention in Chicago as to whether either candidate would support the other.

Considering the ultimate Eisenhower landslide, one may wonder in retrospect why endorsements were important, especially to Eisenhower. It must be remembered that in 1952, polling was far more unreliable than it is today, and after the 1948 upset of Dewey by Truman, there was no room for overconfidence, and therefore the ultimate outcome of the election was far from certain. Although Eisenhower carried 297 congressional districts, Republicans won in only 221 of those districts. Jenner won, while many of Eisenhower's supporters lost.

In his book *My Indiana, Indianapolis Times* reporter Irving Leibowitz describes an interview in August 1952 with Jenner. Jenner made clear that he would not change his views to conform to those of Eisenhower. He said, "Conditions and crisis change, fundamentals never change. I'm going to continue with the same fundamental principles that I've stood by for twenty years." He concluded the interview, however, saying that he expected no public controversy with Eisenhower despite political differences. On August 7, 1952, he released a statement ending any uncertainty, declaring that he, as a loyal Republican, supported Eisenhower despite their "divergence of opinion." Poder's study also states that Jenner affirmed that the Republican Party was "not a goose-stepping regimented chain gang of yes men…" but a party with room for differences.

Dad's support for Eisenhower was made easier by his contempt for the Truman administration and the Korean War. In late August and early September, Jenner condemned our unconditional involvement in the Korean War and reminded Indiana voters that Congress had not declared the Korean War, as required by the Constitution. It had been declared by the United Nations and had become "a bloody treadmill war that the administration won't let us win." Jenner asked, "Must we continue to nail the flower of the youth of this great nation to the cross of Korea?" He believed that Adlai Stevenson was too clearly wed to the Truman administration to end the Korean War and that Eisenhower would bring the courage to the White House to honorably and successfully end it, as the Indianapolis newspapers reported.

Jenner also felt that Eisenhower would be stronger than Stevenson on the communism issue, quipping that "if Adlai gets into the White House, Alger [Hiss, a convicted communist sympathizer] gets out of the jail house" (Poder, p. 119; *Star* August 27 and September 7).

In any event, Jenner and Eisenhower met in Chicago three days before Eisenhower's visit to Indianapolis. At the conference, the two men exchanged warm greetings and were photographed with interlocked arms, according to Poder's account. After the meeting, Jenner announced that they were in close agreement on basic foreign and domestic issues, national defense, the federal budget and inflation. Jenner said, "It was an inspiration to discover that General Eisenhower and I see eye-to-eye on all these major matters ... we are patriotic Americans enlisted in a crusade to save our form of government... ."

If Eisenhower was so opposed to Jenner, it was indeed strange that Jenner was chosen to introduce him to the large crowd at Butler University on September 10, 1952. At the conclusion of the speech, at the request of the photographers, Jenner grasped and raised Eisenhower's hand in the traditional political salute, the action that apparently so appalled Eisenhower's supporters. It is likely that the Indianapolis story was invented by Eisenhower supporters who disliked Jenner.

Senator Carl Curtis remembered in an interview with David Tudor that Jenner could occasionally charm even his enemies. He recalled that President Eisenhower attended a party for the senators and their wives. "Bill Jenner got up and performed ... he could sing and was quite a comedian. Everybody thoroughly enjoyed it." (He probably sang "Red Hot Mama," an old Sophie Tucker song. It goes—"made a music maestro drop his fiddle, made a baldheaded man part his hair in the middle.") "The first thing we realized was not only the President applauding, but he was shouting 'We want Jenner! We want Jenner!'" along with the rest of the party."

The 1952 election saw a great Republican victory in Indiana. Not only did Eisenhower defeat Stevenson for president, but George Craig was elected governor and Jenner was elected U.S. senator. Eisenhower carried Indiana by more than 300,000 votes (58 percent to 41 percent), Craig won by a margin of 55 percent to 43 percent, and Jenner defeated probably the strongest candidate, the popular former Governor Henry F. Schricker, by 52 percent to 46 percent, a margin of more than

100,000 votes. Republicans also elected ten of the 11 congressmen and secured sizable majorities in both houses of the state legislature.

I remember that election day. A newspaperman was at our home on the farm on US 50 east of Bedford. He was there to get Dad's reaction to the election results. He seemed surprised that no one was with Dad except my mother, our cocker spaniel Kelly and me. He observed that Dad was not nervous and kept asking him if he was concerned about the results. Dad did not seem concerned, and I remember no concern on my own part.

I honestly believe that Dad didn't particularly care if he won or lost. He had wanted to be governor, but I believe that being a U.S. senator and spending half the year in Washington, DC, had no great continuing allure for him. Perhaps he felt it was a responsibility, not a calling he eagerly welcomed.

I remember that early that afternoon he received a phone call from Indianapolis. Apparently some machines had breakdowns, and during the repair it was noted that Republicans were winning by a large majority. They asked Dad to come to Indianapolis for the victory celebration. Dad put mother and me in our Buick and we drove to Indianapolis to the Claypool Hotel, where Republicans were enjoying the victory.

It was also a national victory. Republicans captured a majority in the U.S. Senate for the first time since 1932, a period of 20 years. With the majority went the chairmanship of the senate committees. Jenner was selected by the Republican leadership to be chairman of the Senate rules committee. He also served on the finance committee and the Senate judiciary committee, and was chairman of the internal security subcommittee of the judiciary committee.

Dad proved to be a very conscientious senator. From 1944 to August 24, 1958, he was present for 1,643 roll call votes out of 1,781 (more than 96 percent). Twenty-four of the missed votes occurred in 1948 when he was campaigning for governor in Indiana.

Senator Carl Curtis of Nebraska said, "He was very effective. He was able to speak with clarity and conciseness and oftentimes with vigor and also picturesque language." Some senators may not have agreed with him, "but nobody misunderstood what his position was. He could state it very clearly. He was a good investigator, totally reliable…. The other members of the [internal security] committee had high regard for him"

(David Tudor interview with Carl Curtis and Nyles Jackson).

Nyles Jackson, Jenner's administrative assistant, noted in that same interview with David Tudor that Richard Nixon and Jenner were never close. Nixon was a loner and was never a member of the inner circle of the Senate. "That's not true of Jenner. He was right in the thick of it. He was well liked on both sides of the aisle…. He was a lot of fun. He was a good story teller, and most important of all, his word was good."

XII

SECOND TERM

Even though Jenner had supported Taft, he had praise for Eisenhower's first year in office. In an article for *Human Events* in 1953, he thanked the president "for restoring ... dignity to our national government." He praised Eisenhower for his appointments to the cabinet and for replacing the joint chiefs of staff, who he claimed formerly had been subservient to the Dean Acheson state department. Jenner claimed that the Acheson state department was committed to eventual "World Government" where American interests no longer counted.

Jenner generally opposed foreign aid and a bipartisan foreign policy in his speeches. His internal security subcommittee began hearings in the spring of 1953 into communist subversion of American education and colleges. According to Attorney General Herbert Brownell, by November 1953 under the Eisenhower security program, 1,456 persons had been ejected from government service as security risks (*New York Times*, November 8, 1953).

In March 1953 Jenner, as a member of the judiciary committee, proposed that Indiana should be entitled to two additional federal judgeships, one for the southern district and one for the northern district. Jenner reported statistics showing that the two present district court judges, William Steckler in the southern district and Luther Swygert of the northern district (both Democrat appointees), were overworked. Jenner's proposal passed the Senate and the House and was signed by President Eisenhower on February 3, 1954.

1954 was a very busy year for Senator Jenner. It included what would eventually be considered several Republican landmark events in the Hoosier state and eventually the McCarthy censure. His Indiana events would include taking over the Republican central committee in

January, a loss of the same in May and the Holder appointment fight. Nationally he would be involved in the investigative calendar for the subcommittee on internal subversion, the McCarthy censure and the 1954 elections. It was during this year that Jenner finally broke ranks with Eisenhower, initially over the Holder appointment and later on the McCarthy issue.

The year began with a trip to Montreal, Canada, where Jenner and Senator Pat McCarran of Nevada, as members of the Senate internal security subcommittee, interviewed Igor Gouzenko, the former Soviet code clerk who turned informer on Russia's atom spies in 1945. According to the *Washington Times Herald* of December 3, 1953, and January 5, 1954, Gouzenko had been living under an assumed name under police protection in Canada since 1945. Therefore the meeting had to be in secret. Gouzenko had given the subcommittee a sworn affidavit on November 20, 1953, saying he had information on spy rings, presumably in the U.S., which had been ignored by Canada.

After the meeting Jenner announced that his subcommittee would be looking into its ties with South American countries and the state department and agriculture department. "From Gouzenko and Fuchs … we are learning more and more about the tremendous size of the communist conspiracy," he told the *Times* in January.

Jenner spoke on the same day to the Indiana American Legion at the Claypool Hotel. "We intend to destroy the invading army of Soviet Fifth Columnists, and we shall continue in that fight until all our hidden enemies are routed, and our people can turn again to their true interests without fear of a stab in the back," he claimed, as the *Star* reported on January 17. Jenner cited to the Legionnaires the case of Sol Adler, a former U.S. treasury department economist named in hearings before his subcommittee as a one-time member of a Soviet spy ring, who was involved intimately in the Chinese–American negotiations over Chiang Kai-Shek and nationalist China. A proposal to reassign Adler was blocked by Secretary of State George C. Marshall. Sol Adler had served as an aide to General Marshall.

Jenner received a standing ovation from the 500 Legion members for his attacks on Marshall, the *Star* reported on January 17. Jenner charged that Marshall helped rebuild the communist armies in China by trying to persuade Chiang to take communists into his anti-communist government. He accused Marshall of indicating that the U.S. insisted on a truce with the communists.

On April 25, 1954, Jenner again made headlines when he urged that the United States break off all relations with Russia. Russia had just seized the Australian ambassador and his wife. Jenner said, "It is time we quit trying to do business with a bandit government. We continue to sit with them at conference tables while we know they are nothing but bandits ... We should sever relations completely with Russia. We should send all their diplomats home." Jenner further declared, "We cannot go into Asia to continue the white man's colonialism." He advocated helping financially the 600,000 South Korean troops and the 500,000 troops on Formosa in their fight against communism (*Star,* April 25, 1954). However, he opposed sending American troops there.

In addition, Jenner's internal subversion subcommittee was actively holding hearings in Washington and in other cities, and he was making speeches in support of Republicans in the 1954 elections, so that Eisenhower could complete cleaning up "the mess in Washington" (*Ohio State Journal,* October 7). Jenner urged that we not be fooled by the Soviet slogan of "peaceful coexistence" and should sever diplomatic relations with the Soviet Union and thus seal off the spy center in their embassy here. He charged that Stalin had broken his pledge not to interfere in America in exchange for diplomatic recognition by the U.S. in 1933: "They fooled us with that 'phony slogan' twenty-one years ago," and Stalin established spy rings directed by Moscow and their U.S. embassy (*News,* November 13, 1954).

On the home front, on January 30, 1954, a special meeting of the Republican State Central Committee was called. At that meeting it was announced that State Chairman Noland Wright (Governor Craig's choice) had resigned and had been replaced by Paul Cyr of Gary. Cyr was a much-decorated former member of the army. He had spent nine months during World War II behind German lines in France, sabotaging the enemy, leading French guerrilla troops and establishing an underground network. He received the Croix de Guerre four times and the French Legion of Honor. Cyr had been an unsuccessful congressional candidate from Gary. He had run better than any Republican in the heavily Democratic union-dominated 1st District. Winning the admiration of many union members, he promised he would physically fight union goons at political meetings. Supporters of Governor Craig sulked and left a previously scheduled Young Republican cocktail party, the *Times* reported on January 31, 1954. Never before had a governor in Indiana lost control of the party machinery.

In April Senator Homer Capehart joined Jenner in "declaring war" on Craig. The senators blasted Governor Craig and Marion County Republican Chairman H. Dale Brown as "selfish Republican rebels." Some wonder why Capehart teamed with Jenner against an incumbent Republican governor. At this time Indiana governors could serve only one 4-year term. Craig was elected in 1952, and his term as governor therefore would expire in 1956. Capehart's term as U.S. senator would also end in 1956. Capehart feared that Craig would fight him for the U.S. Senate nomination in 1956, and he would need the support of the Jenner faction to prevail. In addition Jenner and Capehart had always had friendly relations and worked in tandem as Republican senators, according to David Tudor's interview with Nyles Jackson and Carl Curtis.

I believe that Dad admired the fact that Capehart was a self-made man who had accumulated a great deal of wealth. Capehart, on the other hand, was impressed by Dad's ability to speak and by his college and law school education. Capehart had not been a college graduate. In addition, Capehart preferred Senate work to building an organization back in Indiana, and therefore he needed the Jenner faction.

They had a long record of cooperation. Capehart had supported Jenner's early unsuccessful 1940 bid for the gubernatorial nomination, and he had also supported Jenner's 1946 Senate bid against incumbent Raymond Willis and his 1948 campaign for the gubernatorial nomination. In 1949 they joined together to elect Cale J. Holder, the youthful 11th District chairman and former chairman of the Republican WWII veterans' group in Marion County, as state chairman, thereby taking control of the Hoosier Republican Party.

These two were also southern Indiana boys and personal friends, and their wives were friendly. Jenner was, however, 11 years younger and philosophically more conservative. After Jenner's retirement Capehart did become more supportive of Eisenhower.

The Craig war was an outgrowth of the struggle between the Taft (Capehart and Jenner) forces and the Eisenhower forces in 1952. At the 1952 state convention Jenner was easily nominated for U.S. Senate on the first ballot, Harold Handley for lieutenant governor on the second ballot and George Craig for governor after three ballots. Taft was clearly the convention's choice for president, electing 30 of the 32 delegates to the national convention. (The complicated rivalries and provocative political actions described in this discussion are based on my own knowledge. They are also covered in Frank Munger's *The Struggle for Republican Leadership in Indiana*.)

It followed, then, that at that January 30, 1954, meeting of the state Republican Central Committee, the Jenner-Capehart forces would have mounted an attempt to take over the committee. They had garnered the support of 14 of the 21 attendee votes and elected Paul Cyr as state chairman. Craig expressed great surprise at the result and termed Cyr's election a coup d'etat. Cyr was only 32 and relatively inexperienced. He was a tough, meaty-looking man whose tactics could be rough enough that Jenner eventually had to part company with him. At the time of his election, however, Cyr was a deputy to Secretary of State Crawford Parker and had at least minimum credentials for the chairmanship. Craig moved forward with his own supporters.

On April 24, 1954, Jenner and Capehart held a joint press conference to denounce Craig's rebel organization. However, Craig, using his main weapon—considerable political patronage—regained control of the party organization on May 12, 1954.

Jenner, with a wide grin, admitted that he had lost the takeover bout, but that all he needed "was a good night's sleep." *Star* columnist Ben Cole on May 16 described Jenner as a fighter but one who "keeps his sense of humor."

The county reorganization meetings of the time were colorful, to say the least. In Martin County, Jenner's companion, Hugh Gray, was re-elected. However, the Craig forces charged that Gray, as chairman of the meeting, refused to let the Craig leaders introduce their candidates, nominated himself, closed the nominations, declared himself the victor on a voice vote and "left so hurriedly that he forgot his hat."

G. T. "Tommy" Fleming Roberts, a mystery story writer of some repute and ally of the Jenner-Capehart forces who later would become bailiff for federal judge Cale J. Holder, was accused of calling a Brown County meeting to order five minutes early, accepting only his own nomination, gaveling it through and then adjourning the meeting. At that time, on cue, a tear gas bomb was exploded outside the door and the electricity was cut off. It is likely, I have been informed, that Cyr was in charge of this "dirty trick." In the darkness, panic and confusion, Roberts exited the meeting and was driven over back roads (to avoid the state police controlled by Governor Craig) to the 9th District meeting, where he cast his vote for Jenner ally Jack Morgan. Politics must have been a lot more exciting and fun in the fifties. These battles are detailed in Frank Munger's *The Struggle for Political Leadership in Indiana.*

In April 1954 in Washington, Jenner continued his plea that we break off all relations with Russia, according to the *Times* of April 25. He blasted the foreign policy of Eisenhower and Dulles as much the same as that of Truman and Acheson. Jenner also was adamant that "American troops should never be sent to Indo-China if the French withdraw." (Clearly he would have opposed the Vietnam War of the 1960s.)

And there was too much vodka drinking going on between American diplomats and the Russians, he said. "What we're doing is dignifying these murderers and bandits who have put much of the world in slavery and still have hopes of doing it to us. By thus dignifying them, we kill every spark of freedom that remains in the hearts of the Russian people, the Latvians, Czechs, Poles and countless others who have been enslaved."

Jenner was being quoted nationally on states' rights when he advocated dismantling the Potomac colossus and returning to private citizens and local government "every activity which can be surrendered by the federal government.When power is surrendered to the federal government" Jenner asserted, we pay in "lost liberties, diminished independence, and in an insidious undermining of our moral fiber and responsibility as a people," he told the *Colorado Springs Gazette-Telegram* on July 23 of this momentous year.

XIII

HOLDER APPOINTMENT AND REPUBLICAN INFIGHTING

Even as a 12-year-old in Washington, I recognized the intensity of the battle Dad waged to have Cale J. Holder appointed as a federal judge in Indiana.

As background to this story, you must understand that Holder had been Republican state chairman in 1952 when General Eisenhower, the "Modern Republican," ultimately defeated Senator Robert Taft, "Mr. Republican," at the Republican national convention in Chicago. As we can recall, Jenner and Holder supported Taft. They also persuaded the Indiana delegation to support Taft by a margin of 30 to 2. (The *Star* editor Eugene Pulliam and Marion County Chairman H. Dale Brown supported Eisenhower.) Because of the bitterness at this convention, Holder refused to move the nomination by acclamation after the Eisenhower victory was assured, and Indiana remained 30 to 2 for Taft. (The convention was sharply divided. Eisenhower only won after allegedly promising a Supreme Court appointment to Earl Warren, governor of California, and after procedural maneuvering wherein "Modern Republicans" unseated traditional black delegates from southern delegations and replaced them with white urban Eisenhower Republicans.)

As a result, Eisenhower was damned if he would appoint Cale Holder to the federal bench. However, another federal judge was badly needed in Indiana. Also, Eisenhower did not count on the power of senatorial courtesy (a Senate tradition whereby the Senate would not approve a federal judge if a senator of the same party from that state objected.) Federal judgeships were one of the few items of patronage that a United States senator had. I remember my father telling me that a township trustee had more patronage than a U.S. senator—a fact that, considering his dislike of federal power—did not displease him. Eisenhower also did not count on the tenacity of Bill Jenner. I remember years later when I clerked for Judge Holder (1966–68), Holder told me that Dad had advised him that he would support him for federal judge because of his service to the Republican Party. Although Holder was a political ally at the time, he was not a close friend, and he was concerned that Eisenhower's opposition might wither Jenner's support. He was concerned that a withdrawal of his name could cause real damage to his legal career. Holder had seen other political endorsements abandoned when things got tough. He, therefore, asked Dad, "Bill, how solid will your support be?" Dad replied, "Cale, I'll stand till blood runs from the crack of my ass." Cale decided that was pretty strong support.

I have never heard that phrase used before or since, but it was the kind of thing Dad would have said and meant. That was the way he expressed himself, but the frank but ingenious crudity hid a sincere commitment. His being so strong in his commitments may have been the reason for his great following among fellow Republicans in the 1940s and 1950s when, for the most part, he dominated the Indiana Republican Party, even though he controlled little patronage. In all I've either read or heard, I don't remember anyone saying Jenner double-crossed them or failed to carry out a promise. Many have said that they didn't like Jenner or his views, but there was never any question as to where he stood on an issue.

Dad had developed an admiration for Holder in the May 1954 fight for control of the state central committee, in which Governor Craig prevailed over the Jenner-Capehart forces. He wrote to Holder on May 21, 1954, thanking him for his support in the losing battle—"you stayed 'hitched' when the going was tough. This is evidence that your convictions were more than mouthwash." Jenner thanked him for his loyalty and commented that "such friends are hard to come by in this life, and I do not soon forget them, nor do I treat their friendship lightly … I want you to remember that whenever I can be of help, you have but to call on me."

In addition, Holder had performed in excellent fashion as state chairman. He took over leadership in 1948 when the party was at a low ebb because of Truman's defeat of Dewey and led the Republican Party to election victories in 1950 and 1952.

Efforts to block Holder's nominations were noted as early as May,

1954. The *Star* reported on May 27 that Governor Craig had "received assurances from the White House that Holder's appointment will not be considered." The same article also reported that "Craig had talked to Attorney General Herbert Brownell about the Holder nomination. Brownell reportedly told Craig he felt he had 'nothing to worry about' and suggested the Governor call Mr. Eisenhower."

It was also noted that these last two federal judge nominees (William Steckler and Holder) had received their law degrees from the Benjamin Harrison Law School (eventually IU law school in Indianapolis) at night. It shocked some of the big-name lawyers in Indianapolis who had graduated from Indiana University Law School at Bloomington or from eastern universities that a couple of hard-working Hoosier night-school boys could attain the prestige of a federal judgeship.

The fight went on for several months. I remember my dad telling me that in the middle of the battle, Eisenhower sent an emissary to meet with him. The emissary said that Eisenhower would appoint Holder if Dad would take back what he said of Eisenhower's friend, General George Marshall. Dad asked the emissary if he had ever read the speech. He admitted he had not, so Dad gave him a copy and asked him to return after he had read it. When he returned, Dad asked what he thought of the speech, and the emissary replied that it was even worse than he had heard, whereupon Dad advised him "to roll the speech up in a tight little ball, take it to Eisenhower and stick it up his ass," as he would not retract a word of the speech. So much for compromise.

Finally, after a long battle, on August 8, 1954, President Eisenhower did nominate Holder to be a federal court judge, despite the opposition of Governor Craig, new state chairman Alvin Cast, and Marion County Republican chairman H. Dale Brown. The deal was struck among Jenner, Ralph Gates, Capehart and Charles Halleck, leaving Craig in the cold, the *Louisville Courier Journal* reported on August 8. The threesome came together on the Holder nomination despite past differences. (Gates as governor personally had managed the "Stop Jenner" 1948 gubernatorial bid, and in 1949 Capehart had blocked Gates from becoming Republican national chairman.)

After his appointment Holder stated his political philosophy in an article in the *Louisville Courier Journal*: "There is only one way to play politics—never quit your team, win, lose or draw." The article noted that many politicians thought Holder had killed his future back in 1952 when he supported Taft and when his forces lost control of the state central committee to Governor Craig in May 1954, "[b]ut it was the team headed by Senators Homer E. Capehart and William E. Jenner, who today are responsible for his appointment as federal judge."

It was reported that both Jenner and Capehart had benefitted politically from this battle: "They demonstrated to the party faithful that, in the clutch, they were loyal to their friends and had the power to get their man the job he wanted ... They are saying even now that 'Bill and Homer delivered when the chips were down.'"

The *Courier Journal* waxed eloquent: "And the odds against which they delivered were extremely impressive to those in the party ranks." They were opposed by the Indiana governor and state Republican chairman, and the President and attorney general of the United States. "Despite the intense pressure that was applied to them to change their minds, they refused to budge . . . The result came in and it showed that Jenner and Capehart could be depended on to keep their word." The article noted that the "Jenner-Capehart victory" had strengthened the hand of Lieutenant Governor Harold Handley in his bid for the nomination for governor in 1956.

The alliance of Jenner, Capehart, Halleck and Gates would create a power-laden coalition. The article observed that Craig's backers had boasted that he would build a "machine the like-of-which has never been seen in Indiana." Craig had started his term quickly to build such a machine, seeking in the 1953 legislature to center vast powers in the hands of the governor. "Only the determined battle of the Jenner-Capehart bloc of state senators prevented the enactment of the Craig program to centralize the state government," the paper opined.

The Craig-Jenner feud continued into 1955. Craig had promised not to run against Capehart in 1956, and therefore Capehart was moving more to the center.

Early in 1955 Jenner joined with other Republicans (William Knowland of California and Styles Bridges of New Hampshire) to oppose the administration's apparent unwillingness to negotiate with communist China over the islands of Quemoy and Matsu without nationalist China being at the table. Jenner charged that appeasers were trying to convince Eisenhower to surrender the islands. Jenner charged that the palace guard around Eisenhower was attempting to mislead the president. Jenner declared that secret groups were attempting to influence U.S. foreign policy (*Times*, February 14 and March 17, 1955).

Craig took up the gauntlet that had been thrown. He saw this as an attack on Eisenhower's foreign policy but more importantly as an opportunity to further ingratiate himself with Eisenhower and the so-called "modern" wing of the Republican Party. In May 1955 Craig called Jenner "neurotic" and stated that Jenner's "second guessing Eisenhower is not unlike an elementary school pupil second guessing Einstein."

Jenner retorted that he was shocked that the governor had issued a statement on foreign policy and added, "Governor Craig has served as the monkey's paw for the palace guard. He has no background in foreign policy. He is in over his head. I do not mind Governor Craig being a monkey in Indiana. The people of Indiana know him. But I do mind his being made a monkey of us in Washington" (*Washington Evening Star*, May 3, 1955).

These were strong words between a Republican governor and a United States senator from the same state. What the two factions were pointing for was the control of the party and the nominations for governor at the June 1956 state convention.

The Jenner faction was backing Lieutenant Governor Handley, a fraternity brother of Jenner's at IU. The Craig faction found Handley unacceptable; Craig planned to control the state organization and build a strong machine to back his political aspirations. Craig had some powerful weapons—patronage, money and control of the state organization. Jenner, on the other hand, had "great personal loyalty to the senator on the part of many persons" (*Evansville Courier*, April 2, 1955).

Why did Jenner have such personal loyalty? He had little or no patronage and no great wealth or wealthy backers. I've said earlier I believe it was because he had a certain charisma formed from many attractive personal characteristics. Beyond that, loyalty. If Bill Jenner said he was for you, he meant it. I never heard of him betraying a former ally for his own political gain.

The journalist Irving Leibowitz said, "If Jenner was your friend, he would lead you through Hell. If you were his enemy, he would push you through it."

Ed Zeigner, the *News*'s political reporter, in 1957 called Jenner a "bare knuckles political grenadier, who has been top Republican banana most of the time since the end of World War II … For reasons hard to analyze, Jenner commands an almost fanatical loyalty from a sizable part of the Republican regulars." Zeigner noted that Jenner had been opposed by Governors Gates and Craig, but he had eclipsed Gates in power and influence, and that by 1957 Craig didn't even live in Indiana anymore. But that is ahead of the story.

Although Eugene Pulliam and the powerful Indiana Republican Editorial Association never liked or supported Jenner, the reporters seemed to like him, charmed by his personal and political talents and strength of conviction. Usually favorable coverage by Irving Leibowitz, Dan Kidney, Ed Zeigner and Ben Cole continued into the 1950's.

The March 7, 1955, *Time* featured a picture of George Craig, Indiana governor, on the cover. The feature article was "At the nation's crossroads, a political collision." The article discussed the factional fight between the forces of Governor Craig and Senator William Ezra Jenner, GOP kingpin since 1944, "who stands at the core of the GOP element that opposed Eisenhower … in 1952 and still opposes him much of the time." The article described Craig, a former national commander of the American Legion, as "a swift-footed, swashbuckling lawyer-politician …." The article was very favorable to Governor Craig, who had been praised by Eisenhower as one "who should be pushed upward and forward in the Eisenhower-led GOP." Jenner was described as having spent more than 20 years shouting and shoving his way upward, throughout the state senate, into the state chairmanship of his party and on to the U.S. Senate. The article praised Craig's leadership as governor in the field of mental health, where he had appointed psychiatrist Margaret Morgan (sister of Jenner ally and 9th District chairman Ivan "Jack" Morgan) as head of the new Mental Health Division, and for his $280 million bond issue to build toll roads in Indiana.

The article described how the Jenner forces captured control of the Indiana Republican Central Committee while Craig was governor. It was very unusual for a sitting governor to lose control of the state committee because of the patronage the governor enjoyed. The Craig forces it will be remembered, were furious and formed their own state committee. It went on to specify Craig's close advisers as Doc Sherwood and Doxie Moore, appointed as his administrative assistant, as Legionnaire pals. The article concluded by stating that in the toe-to-toe struggle between Jenner and Craig, Craig clearly had the good wishes and help of President Eisenhower.

But these henchmen, close to George Craig, were heading for a fall, and that fall in a couple of years would implicate the governor of the state also. Virgil "Red" Smith had been appointed by Craig as highway commission chairman and the trouble would involve Smith. Apparently insiders would purchase land they knew would be taken by the state for highway purposes and then receive much larger payments from the state when the land was actually taken. The Marion County grand jury handed down specific indictments on Thursday, May 2, 1957. The *Times*, which had reported so many political ups and downs of George Craig, recorded on May 5 that those indicted were Smith; Robert Peak, attorney and friend of Smith, for false negotiation and grand larceny; Nile Tevenbaugh, former right-of-way chief, for embezzlement of public funds and grand larceny; and Harry Doggett, Greensburg, a close friend of Craig's and former assistant right-of-way chief, for conspiracy to commit a felony, to wit grand larceny. Further, on June 23, 1957, a Marion County grand jury held Craig "morally, if not legally, responsible for the acts and misconducts of the high officials he selected." The prosecutor at this time was John G. Tinder of Marion County. (His son, John Tinder, was later to become United States district attorney, a United States district court judge and finally a judge on the U.S. court of appeals for the 7th Circuit in Chicago.)

Maurice A. Hutcheson, who inherited the carpenters' union from William (Big Bill) Hutcheson, was also involved. Hutcheson was one of the few Indiana Republicans to support Dewey over Taft in 1948 and Eisenhower over Taft in 1952.

An article in *Look* concluded in its December 10, 1957 issue that "[t]he Eisenhower team in Washington had eyed Craig as the man to unhorse Jenner for the 1958 Republican senatorial nomination, but now Craig lies almost fatally wounded politically." And—"one thing seems certain. The next senator from Indiana will not be an Eisenhower Republican. Ex-Governor Craig's underlings saw to that."

Earlier on January 13, 1957, Jenner and former governor Ralph Gates (now allies) and Governor Handley took control of the Republican Party from Craig and Halleck, ousting Al Cast as state chairman, Tom Mahaffey as treasurer and Mrs. Von L. Snyder as state vice chairman. Capehart also joined in the movement. Morgan, an ally of Jenner, was elected 9th District chairman, replacing a Craig supporter who resigned. Mrs. Frank Pope, vice chairman of the 9th District and my mother's maid of honor, replaced Craig supporter Alma Burke of Vevay. Another Craig supporter, 10th District chairman, Russell Robbins, also resigned, giving Jenner and the Gates forces a likely 15 votes out of the 22, according to the *Times* on January 13, 1957.

The election as state chairman of Jenner ally Robert Matthews, who held no brief for Eisenhower's New Republicanism, had effectively ended the influence of ex-governor Craig on the Indiana Republican Party. The highway scandal indictments sealed his fate and ended his polical career. According to Nyles Jackson, Jenner's administrative assistant, Jenner didn't dislike Craig but felt sorry for him. Jenner was reported to have said to Jackson, "Nyles, some of those darn guys around him are going to get that guy in jail … I know 'em and I've known 'em for years … I don't think George knew who he was dealing with" (Jackson interview with David Tudor).

XIV

JENNER AND MCCARTHY AND THE
COMMUNIST INVESTIGATIONS

Histories tend to lump Jenner and Senator Joseph McCarthy together in the congressional investigations of communist infiltration in America. Bill Jenner was a friend of McCarthy. He liked him, regarding him as a prototypical Irishman who loved to drink, gamble and go to the races. However, Jenner joined the Senate internal security subcommittee in 1946, long before McCarthy became interested in the issue of communism. Jenner regarded the issue as one best handled by the internal security subcommittee and felt that McCarthy, who in 1953 was chairman of the government operations subcommittee, was operating beyond his jurisdiction. Neither senator worked in concert with the other, as the committees were totally separate entities. Although McCarthy made his Wheeling, West Virginia, speech in February of 1950, his influence in Congress lasted only during his term as chairman of the government operations committee's permanent subcommittee on investigations, a period of less than two years (1952–54). McCarthy was censured by the Senate on December 2, 1954, which completely ended his influence.

Jenner, ever loyal to his friends, was one of the leaders of the anti-censure group and voted against the censure in 1954. When McCarthy died on May 2, 1957, Jenner was one of three U.S. senators to accompany his casket from Washington, DC, to his burial place in Appleton, Wisconsin. Jenner was quoted as saying, "I've been his friend this long; I'm not going to leave him now." Robert F. Kennedy also attended McCarthy's funeral.

It has been noted that in the field of internal subversion, "the far more knowledgeable and competent house committee on un-American activities …, and the subcommittee on internal security, … McCarthy played no role in either—produced an immense body of evidence, collected at hearings and set down in reports. The printed hearings of these two subcommittees remain an invaluable resource, particularly in the continuing efforts to place new revelations in perspective," according to the book *The Verona Secrets*, by Herbert Romerstein and Eric Breindel.

Every report issued by the Senate internal security subcommittee while Jenner was chairman was endorsed unanimously by all members of the subcommittee, Republican and Democrat. The subcommittee's report, entitled "Interlocking Subversion in Government," was accepted as an excellent study of how the communists had infiltrated the government.

Jenner's subcommittee on internal subversion strictly followed a standard procedure. The subcommittee took, in executive session, the testimony of responsible ex-communists and reliable government agents. The evidence was carefully assessed and corroborated before the person identified as a communist was subpoenaed. The testimony was not made public until the persons identified as communists were given an opportunity in private session to deny the evidence. The names of those who denied communist affiliation were not brought into the public hearings. However, if they refused to deny or controvert the evidence, a public hearing followed.

Investigations had revealed that the largest group of underground communists were college professors. Jenner was clear, however, when he stated at the outset of the hearings, "Our purpose is to protect and safeguard academic freedom ... The free market of ideas cannot function if hidden conspirators are waiting ... to attack and destroy the loyal people teaching our youth ... Our committee is not concerned with telling the leaders of our schools and colleges what to teach or how to teach. It is concerned with showing them where this alien conspiracy is hidden ... It's concerned with helping our academic leaders to meet the threat," as Robert Morris records of these events in his book *No Wonder We Are Losing*.

Senator Prescott Bush of Connecticut, the father of a future president and grandfather of another, stated, "I recall particularly that the distinguished senator from Indiana was commended by many persons, both those who agreed with him and those who did not, for the way in which he conducted the hearings ... I recall particularly a statement by R. Harry D. Gideonese of Brooklyn College in which he specifically said that … the senator from Indiana had conducted those hearings with eminent fairness to all concerned." Jenner was clear that his subcommittee was to undertake their investigations with the view of "preventing further infiltration and not to hold up or pillory past misdeeds."

Since the great majority of the communist infiltration occurred during World War II when the Russians were "allies," Democrats and liberals generally looked with great disfavor on the investigations because they tended to discredit the Roosevelt and Truman administrations. An example occurred in November 1953, when Eisenhower's attorney general, Herbert Brownell, announced that President Truman had promoted Harry Dexter White to the International Monetary Fund in 1945, even though White's spying activities for the Soviet Union "were reported in detail by the FBI to the White House … ." Truman immediately shot back misstatements that he couldn't remember seeing any FBI reports mentioning White and upon reflection, said, "As soon as we knew he was disloyal, we fired him." And then, in a later television address, he added a new misstatement of fact—that he had first learned of charges against White in February 1946 and had tried to stop White's appointment but found that the Senate had already confirmed White.

In an unprecedented appearance on November 17, 1953, FBI Director J. Edgar Hoover, accompanied by Attorney General Brownell, appeared before the Senate subcommittee on internal security chaired by Jenner. First Brownell read into the records FBI reports on Harry Dexter White, who was by then deceased. Hoover, after being introduced by Jenner to loud applause as "the custodian of the nation's security," followed with a statement, the clear import of which essentially branded Truman as a liar as well as being incredibly naïve. It was no wonder that Truman had few good things to say about Jenner or Hoover. The case against White and Truman's part in it is reported in the book *J. Edgar Hoover: The Man and the Secrets* by Curt Gentry.

XV

U.S. SENATE AND INDIANA POLITICS

We need to return a couple of years to the time before George Craig's debacle and fall in 1957. Jenner was in his second term in Washington and was continuing to criticize so-called bipartisan foreign policy. Truman, in a speech at French Lick in the fall of 1955, in essence said that people cannot be expected to understand foreign policy—a job that should be left to the experts. Jenner, for his part, had believed that the 1952 election was a mandate for Eisenhower to change the direction of American foreign policy. He charged that once the new president had been sworn in, changes had not been made and that the policies of Eisenhower and John Foster Dulles were not essentially different than those of Truman and Dean Acheson. He continued to feel that way. The *Times* on January 22, 1956, devoted an editorial, "Sen. Jenner speaks his piece," to these foreign policy charges. However, in 1958, Jenner backed Dulles against detractors and received a personal thank you from Dulles. Dad responded that Dulles was paying the price anyone has to pay when they stand up against communism. "You can't sit down with gangsters, thieves, murderers and liars and do business."

Back in Indiana, however, Jenner scored the greatest political victory of his career. Jenner backed his ally, Lieutenant Governor Harold W. Handley, for governor. Craig was out to stop Handley at any cost, having declared that Handley was unacceptable and that he preferred any of four other candidates: Frank T. Millis, a former Jenner ally; John Scott of South Bend; Frank Sparks of Crawfordsville; and Dan Cravens of Franklin. Craig predicted that Millis would have upwards of 700 votes on the first ballot and that together the four would have the delegates to stop Handley, according to the *Star*.

Jenner was in Indianapolis for the convention to be held at the state fairgrounds on June 29, 1956. Followers of Hoosier politics were interested in the fact that Governor Ralph Gates was on the Jenner team. Congressman Charles Halleck also arrived before the convention to circulate among the delegates on behalf of Craig's "Stop Handley" program. Craig, as governor, and his forces had control of arrangements for the fairgrounds site. The hall was draped with huge pictures of Eisenhower, Craig and Homer Capehart, but, insultingly, none of Jenner.

In spite of all this hoopla, Handley won a resounding victory. His victory was a crushing defeat for Craig and his forces and showed the ever-strong support for the senator from southern Indiana and his conservative agenda. During the proceedings, Craig was booed by the party delegates, chanting, "We want Jenner." Jenner ascended to the podium and declared it was "[t]he end of a perfect day." It was probably the most dramatic ending to a Republican state convention ever. Leibowitz in the *Times* described the ovation that Jenner received as "one of the most exciting and sentimental, in the long and turbulent history of Indiana political conventions." It was the precursor to the scandals which would follow next year.

I believe this was the inception in Dad's mind of his decision to leave politics. Governor had been his goal, surely strongly influenced by his father's wishes, but Woody had died in 1950, so that was probably no longer goading him on. Dad did not like Washington, and though he had many friends in the Senate, he was not truly fond of the legislative process. In fact his poor vision prevented his close attention to the details of legislation. Since the end of World War II, he had gradually experienced dimming eyesight. His speeches were printed in large type.

Still, at this point he was the kingpin of Indiana Republican politics and had been for the better part of the post-war years. His friend and fraternity brother would be governor. If Jenner's plan had worked, he would have succeeded him as U.S. senator. In addition he was truly a party man and did not enjoy opposing Eisenhower on a great number of issues. It was not easy to turn the direction of the Ship of State, and he had found that out.

From 1956 through 1958, although he fought increasingly hard against the trends of one-worldism and the diminishment of American power and political morality, he seemed to find only frustration as he viewed the ongoing drift to feckless liberalism and economic irresponsibility in Washington.

During the Roosevelt and Truman times, he had attributed the leftward direction of the nation to Democrat New Dealers and Fair Dealers. He thought that a Republican administration would stop the increase in federal power and spending and the one-world trend he feared. Instead he felt that Eisenhower, by continuing many of the domestic and foreign policies of the former administrations, merely entrenched and gave wider currency and legitimization to those policies.

In a speech in Chicago, he said that the presidency was being given too much power, the autocratic, transcendent ruling ability of an emperor. "The office is being changed from the American constitutional office of First Citizen of the Republic ... .The President is pictured as an indispensible man. He is credited with sole responsibility for decisions and achievements that a superman could not make," the *Washington Post and Times Herald* quoted Jenner as saying on February 12, 1956.

In January 1956 he had switched from the rules committee to the Senate finance committee. He made the switch to help Chairman Harry F. Byrd (D, Virginia) to "hold down taxes and keep a ceiling on the national debt." He also was serving on the judiciary committee and the post office and civil service committees.

Jenner continued to campaign on the theme that "we shall escape the swamps of the New Deal and come into the light of liberty, when our states decide they are masters in their own house and ... tell the national government what to do," the *Bedford Daily Times* reported on November 3. However, the article pointed out, he continued to disagree with his own party over foreign aid and foreign policy.

The final and decisive split with Eisenhower came over the Hungarian Revolution in late 1956. Jenner was "shocked" because the United States did not take stronger action against Soviet intervention in the Hungarian Revolution. He argued that "pompous words" were no deterrent to Russia. In the *Ft. Wayne News Sentinel* for November 28, Jenner stated, "this is the last chance to decide whether the United Nations has any moral significance ...." Jenner argued that if the UN did not bring Russia to the bar of world justice and denounce its attack on unarmed Hungarians, it would no longer be relevant to Hoosiers. Introduced at the Indiana Society meeting held in Chicago in December as "Indiana's fighting senator," he received the most enthusiastic reception, Irving Leibowitz reported in the *Times.*

Jenner continued to speak against increasing the national debt, calling it as big a threat to the survival of the United States as that of communism.

On May 11, 1957, Vice President Richard Nixon and his wife Pat visited Indiana. Nixon, described inaccurately as a personal friend of Jenner, gave the assembled newsmen the impression that "[b]oth President Eisenhower and Vice President Nixon will back Senator William E. Jenner if he is re-nominated next year." He declared that Jenner had backed most of Eisenhower's domestic programs, and that Jenner's opposition to foreign aid was a matter of principle on which Jenner had been unwavering and was therefore understandable, according to the *Star's* coverage of the event.

Robert Matthews, a Jenner and Handley man, was state chairman and declared that the party needed Jenner in 1958, according to the *Times* on May 5. "The fact is that Jenner represents the thinking of the people in Indiana, especially on ending foreign aid and curtailing big spending."

In an October 11, 1956, article, Jenner had outlined the points in which his positions diverged from those of the Eisenhower administration: "I am wholly opposed to foreign aid, GATT, UNESCO, NATO and to any assumption of sovereign ... powers by the United Nations." For such beliefs Jenner had been called an "unappeasable" in a October 26, 1956, article in *Colliers* by "Modern Republican" Paul Hoffman, who opined that Jenner had no place in the new Republican Party that Eisenhower was trying to build. It was typical of the liberal criticism that followed Jenner throughout his life and political career.

There was no question that prior to the May 1957 indictments, of the Craig lieutenants, Craig and Halleck were plotting to "drop Jenner" and take control of the Republican state committee, so alleged the *Times* in articles in February 1957. It was thought that Craig or Halleck might oppose Jenner for the Senate nomination at the 1958 convention. One Indiana congressman said that such a course would not be wise: "Jenner has a fanatical following among Republicans. If he is defeated in the convention, those same people will either stay home or vote Democratic."

Although it was no secret that many Eisenhower supporters wanted to be rid of Jenner, for his part Jenner pointed to his voting record, claiming he had backed the President on most votes and only opposed him on foreign aid and the Bricker amendment. One of the pro-Eisenhower Indiana congressmen conceded that Jenner was correct, but explained, "When I oppose the President I ... do it politely and with respect and deference to him. When Jenner votes with the President he always manages to call him an SOB" (*Times*, February 17). In fact, Jenner's voting record as compiled by the *Congressional Quarterly* showed him supporting Eisenhower's policies in his second term 85.2 percent of the time. Halleck had a record of 82.4 percent support and Capehart only 64.7 percent.

Eisenhower suffered a heart attack in September 1955, which fueled speculation that he might not run in 1956. When Dad was asked his thoughts by a reporter, his response was, "Hell, we'll stuff him and run him."

In February 1957 Jenner again found himself opposed to Eisenhower on the issue of federal aid to education. Jenner felt that states could provide for their educational needs as they had done since the founding of the republic. He saw this as an attempt to put the "federal camel under the tent of our local school systems."

Also in January 1957, the *Times* had shown Jenner defending cloture in debate on the Senate floor, declaring the concept of free debate to be as important as the concept of majority rule. "Free debate has deterred power-seeking executives from seeking legislation which is too dictatorial," Jenner contended. He declared that Christ was killed by a majority and Christians were tortured, noting "[t]he American people have a constitutional right to be heard before their money is voted or their liberty restrained ...."

In January 1957 a large delegation from Indiana attended Eisenhower's inauguration. Jenner hosted a buffet in the Senate Office Building for the entire Hoosier delegation. However, trouble was brewing. Eisenhower proposed in 1957 "the biggest peacetime budget in history." Jenner was strong in his opposition; after all, he had joined the powerful Senate finance committee to help Harry Byrd cut the budget. Jenner declared, "The spenders will never give up their spending until they are compelled by a political force stronger than the spending agencies and their propaganda arms."

He also attacked a recommendation by the commission on government security that five-year prison terms and heavy fines be levied on reporters who printed material marked "secret" by a bureau head. He noted ironically that the communists seemed to be able to learn our secrets. "This ... is a direct road to dictatorship. A petty bureau head can put the stamp of secrecy on a document to cover up its own crimes. It amounts to complete censoring of the press," the *Star* reported on June 25, 1957.

The *Times* reported Jenner also urged the government to withdraw its 80,000 troops from the Korean "death trap" because across the line there were 450,000 North Koreans and 350,000 Red Chinese troops ready to attack.

The proposed Eisenhower budget of $72 billion was facing cuts, and the cuts were generally popular, prompting Eisenhower to sometimes side with the cutters. This made it difficult for Congressman Halleck, who was the Eisenhower floor leader. The *Times* on April 21, 1957, stated it was similar to the time when the late James Watson was President Hoover's floor leader and the White House switched sides in the middle of a floor fight. Watson remarked, "How you gonna' stand behind a man with St. Vitus Dance?"

Jenner made no secret of his opposition to Eisenhower's brand of modern Republicanism, declaring that the Grand Old Party "is good enough for me." Jenner snidely declared that he was no Modern Republican, "because his parents had been married." He received criticism from Eisenhower and other Republicans, and even the *London Economist*, which decried the Senate seniority system that "brings Senator Jenner of Indiana, a foaming reactionary against President Eisenhower and all his words to the crucial senate finance committee, which handles ... such matters as American membership in the organization for trade cooperation—and the British request for a waiver of interest on the American loan."

On June 14, 1957, in a two-hour Senate speech, Jenner blasted foreign aid, calling it "new colonialism." He was responding to the new Eisenhower plan, dividing defense expenditures from economic aid and putting the latter on a loan basis. Jenner said the loans would not be repaid and called it "foreign aid folly." It's the "same old girl in a new dress," he charged in the *Times* of June 14, 1957. Jenner strongly believed that our foreign aid was meant to invade the sovereignty of the recipient nations, and that each nation should be able to set conditions regarding the aid so as to protect its sovereignty and political institutions.

In his last speech on the Senate floor on August 21, 1958, he said, "Our country is not governed by officials in the Capitol.... Its strength will be in the country, not in the Capitol. Its political sovereignty will lie with the people, not in the officials. Its intellectual energy will be widespread in all parts of the nation, not emanating in a cloud from Washington. Its spirit and strength will be in its families, its local communities, its local papers, its local schools and colleges, and symphony orchestras and baseball sand lots."

Much later he gave similar advice during a campaign to a group of Republican politicos, showing the consistency of his opinions. The microphone was unintentionally left on, and reporters, including one from the *Evansville Press*, March 20, 1985 heard Jenner say, "Forget the fucking cities. Concentrate on the farms and the towns. We've got the most conservative press and the most conservative people in America. Pour it on. Call the Democrats dupes, dopes, pinks and finks."

XVI

POLICY POSITIONS

It is appropriate at this point to take a detailed look at Jenner's policy stands while he was in the United States Senate. It is certain that he could not be boxed into any one labeled party position or stand dictated from above but was always "his own man."

A. Civil Rights

Researchers were often surprised about Jenner's approach to civil rights. Thomas Kotulak, an IU Southeast professor of political science, in *Scribner's Encyclopedia of American Lives*, wrote, "when Indiana high schools would not allow black schools to participate in the State basketball tournament, Jenner helped push through the State senate a bill opening the tournament to all public and parochial schools … When it came to civil rights, he seemed to take some unpopular stands for the time."

Bill Jenner was a strong advocate of civil rights. On December 5, 1945, when he was Republican state chairman, he gave a speech in Indianapolis that was later distributed by the Republican Veterans of Indiana as a pamphlet describing what he felt the Republican Party should stand for on the issue of civil rights. He wrote:

"We must recognize that the Negroes in America have suffered more and enjoyed less security for a longer time than any group in our Nation. This we must reverse and remedy, not by charity, but by the dignity of opportunity for leadership and self improvement."

When he served in the state legislature, Indiana high schools prohibited African American schools from participating in the state basketball tournament. Jenner helped push through the state senate a bill opening the tourney to all public and parochial schools regardless of race or religion. State Senator Robert Brokenburr, son of a slave, who became an alternate delegate to the United Nations and was one of the most respected black civil leaders in Indiana, credited Jenner with helping to break down Jim Crow barriers in Indiana. Irving Leibowitz, a Jew and admirer of Jenner, noted in his book *My Indiana* that Jenner had waged and won over the powerful protest of *Indianapolis Star* publisher Eugene Pulliam and President Eisenhower a battle to have Cale Holder, a Catholic, appointed federal judge.

When Jenner came to the United States Senate in 1946, no civil rights legislation existed for African Americans. It was impossible to secure passage of even federal anti-lynching statutes because of southern opposition. Jenner once asked for unanimous consent to consider an anti-lynching bill, saying, "I see there are no Democrats on the floor. This would be a good time to pass this part of the civil rights program."

In 1950 he introduced an amendment to the Railway Labor Act to prohibit discrimination against blacks in railroad unions. It therefore was not surprising that he voted for the 1957 Civil Rights Act. This law, the first civil rights legislation since Reconstruction, gave the federal government the power to seek injunctions against limitations or denials of voting rights of African Americans and established the civil rights commission. He endorsed the Civil Rights Act because it guaranteed the right to vote protected by the Fifteenth Amendment and "was needed to preserve the spirit of our laws that gave equality to all citizens regardless of race or color," as Michael Poder summarizes in his study covering Jenner's views on civil rights.

I remember as a 10-year-old during the 1952 election campaign attending black church services in Indianapolis with my father and mother and noting the sincerity of the affection the large congregation seemed to feel for him. I also remember my father telling me that the communists had felt that the blacks of America would be a rich recruiting ground for them, but they had been disappointed. He felt that their basic family values and belief in God had prevented any mass movement of African Americans to atheistic communism.

He believed that Democrats' promises to blacks were merely "vote bait," with no commitment to progress to ease their plight. He felt Democrats' insincerity was evidenced by the failing of the Truman administration to force southern Democrats to support civil rights legislation.

B. The Constitution, Limited Government and Executive Power

Jenner believed that the principles of the founding fathers embodied in the Constitution were fundamental truths as appropriate for the modern day as they had been for an earlier United States. He specifically outlined his views on constitutional government in a pamphlet, "What Has Happened To Our Country, A Summing Up," stating, "I propose that we in this country go back wholly, completely, and immediately to the principles on which this country was founded."

Because education was not an enumerated power of the federal government, Jenner opposed federal spending and involvement in education. In 1958 he opposed the National Defense Education Act as an unwarranted intrusion of federal power into state and local school systems. There was no Department of Education in the federal government at that time. Later, President Ronald Reagan would advocate abolition of the Department of Education.

In 1949 Jenner complained that the indebtedness of the United States amounted to more than the combined national debts of all Marshall Plan recipients, as Rodney Ross reports. He lamented the perpetual borrowing of money and the consequent mutual obligation and the depreciation of the American dollar as "indebted inflation." He pointed out that "more than ten percent of our budget is used to pay interest on our national debt."

As Poder reports, Jenner's first Senate speech dealt with the necessity of restoring governmental efficiency and a reduction in federal expenditures. He described taxes as the "master switch of government power" and argued that increased federal spending strengthened centralized political control and undermined the states, reducing them to the status of lackeys and "provinces of Washington." Big government, he argued, required heavy taxation and deficit spending to perpetuate itself, and these policies encouraged dependence on national authority. Jenner decried what he regarded as the usurpation of state sovereignty by the federal government: "[W]e look now to the federal government for the solution to most of our problems. Problems which traditionally have been met by the state and local governments, or private initiative…." He regretted that legislation had permitted "attempts to glorify the Presidency and change it into an office never envisioned by the Constitutional Convention," allowing it to become superior to Congress in weight and influence.

Jenner believed that massive government spending, the growth of a huge bureaucracy, government secrecy and the perversion of the treaty power had enabled a small elite in the executive branch to gain unconstitutional control of the national government. He lamented the notion that the presidency was "a mystical center of absolute power to be occupied by a super-human person to whom all things can be entrusted without question" (Poder). Jenner had no great love of the presidency, or President Truman, or President Eisenhower. He once said that President Truman enjoyed attending football games because it was a relief to watch someone else fumble.

C. Free Trade

In 1947 the United States entered into the General Agreement on Tariffs and Trade (GATT), the forerunner of the World Trade Organization (WTO). Article 1, Section 8, of the Constitution provides that "The Congress shall have power...to regulate commerce with foreign nations." Jenner said that "the international regulations and administrative machinery of GATT ... have never been submitted to Congress for approval or rejection" (Congressional Record 84th Congress, Senate, 1955.) As Ross noted, "[Jenner] attacked the state department for exaggerating the benefits and ignoring the evils of the reciprocal trade agreement legislation. State department offices ignored the intent of congress to protect American labor and industry as they promoted a campaign to open the United States to the inexpensive goods of foreign workers and interest" (Congressional Record 85th Congress, Senate, 1958).

Jenner insisted that GATT was a "system for the export of jobs." Between 1947 and 1958, he supported bills and amendments protecting domestic industrial and agricultural products. His arguments sound much like those put forward today against unlimited free trade. He said, "this international body (GATT) is not concerned primarily with free trade ... but with its very opposite, an elaborate worldwide system of quotas and allocation of markets which is under no obligation to put American interests above those of 35 other members" (Congressional Record, 85th Congress, Senate, 1958).

XVII

DECISION TO RETIRE

In December 1957 Jenner dropped a bombshell in a letter to Republican State Chairman Robert Matthews. Both the *Times* and the *Chicago Tribune* on December 1 declared that Jenner was announcing he would not be a candidate for re-election in 1958. He stated that he and his family would return to Indiana, and that he would open a law practice in the Illinois Building in Indianapolis with former United States District Attorney Jack C. Brown. The decision was no surprise to Mother and me. We had moved to a home located at 1307 "O" Street in Bedford in the summer of 1957, and I enrolled that fall as a sophomore at Bedford High School.

The next day Jenner said that "personal" not "political" reasons prompted his move. The announcement was reported by the *Star* to have "stunned the political world … On both sides of the political fence leaders admitted that Jenner was virtually assured of a third senate term if he chose to run." Jenner for his part was in high spirits and preparing to leave on a quail-hunting trip.

Democratic National Chairman Paul Butler greeted the decision as "good news" for Democrats. The *Times* reported Butler as saying, "In Indiana Jenner would have been tougher than any man to beat," and that Jenner's departure from the scene enhanced Democrat chances in the state. The article went on to describe him as one of the "most colorful" senators in Washington. Jenner's pet dislikes were international spending, communism and what he termed a one-world scheme.

Why had Jenner done this at the height of a successful career?

Long-time friend and fishing buddy Hugh Gray told the paper that he got the impression that Jenner wanted to stay home with his family and son Billy.

Irving Leibowitz theorized that Jenner had been discouraged when senators like conservative Everett Dirksen of Illinois supported the large Eisenhower budget. Leibowitz noted that Jenner was warned by a Senate colleague in 1950 not to take the floor to oppose George Marshall as secretary of defense. "The press will cut you to ribbons. Marshall is a great war hero," said the colleague. Jenner looked him in the eye and said, "I am expendable. It would be a sorry thing if … a man in public life can't tell the truth for fear of newspapers which are involved in a conspiracy not to tell the truth." Leibowitz summed up his article with a quote from Jenner's friend, Hugh Gray: "Bill never forgets a friend—or an enemy."

Most newspapers in Indiana expressed regret that he was retiring, including, for example, the *Richmond Times Dispatch, Marion Chronicle, Kokomo Tribune, Richmond Palladium, Bedford Daily Times Mail* and *Madison Courier.* Of course the national liberal dailies, the *Washington Post* and the *Christian Science Monitor,* could hardly control their glee. However, even Jenner's critics conceded that his committee work on the Senate rules committee and the internal security subcommittee earned him universal respect.

The Democrat-leaning *Louisville Courier-Journal* editorialized that the 49-year-old Jenner had written himself a foolproof insurance policy, arguing that if the Republicans lost in '58, there would be a great cry for his return, and if they won he would be making money in a lucrative law practice. There was also speculation that he would run for governor in 1960.

Jenner broke his silence on December 22, 1957, in an interview with the *Times.* In the interview he admitted that he was fed up with bureaucratic Washington and fighting "modern Republicans," but those are excuses—not reasons. He said, "I want Billy to have a home town. I want him to belong. I want him to have someplace to call home when I'm gone. I want him to finish high school in Bedford. I want him to be able to walk down the street and know people. If my boy is … a scrub on the football team … if it's Dad's Day … I'm gonna be there. He's gonna have the next three years of my life."

It is a little daunting to think that he gave up a still-promising political career at age 49 for me. Still, I do think that it may have indeed been the central reason. Mother and Dad believed that I should have roots. I have enjoyed those roots in Bedford, at Indiana University, and in my 45 years of law practice in Madison, so their wishes in that respect and Dad's surprising stand to leave the Senate have paid off. Also, I know my parents had no liking for the Washington social scene. I could count on two hands the number of times I had a sitter so that they could attend a social event. Our home life consisted of dinner, homework and watching television together.

As Ed Zeigner of the *News* wrote, it was unusual to retire when you were on top. Gates had stopped Jenner in 1948, as had Craig for a time in the '50s prior to the road scandals, but as Zeigner noted, Gates was eclipsed by Jenner now, and Craig, politically feeble, didn't even live in Indiana. Fulton Lewis, Jr. wrote in his nationally syndicated *Washington Report* that there was only one reason Jenner retired, and that was his desire to be with his wife and child, "which merely proves how great a man the senator is."

Having announced his retirement in 1957, Jenner was somewhat of a lame-duck senator in 1958. However, he participated actively in the 1958 campaign, which turned out badly for the Republican Party. He made his last speech in Bedford at the auditorium. Jenner always made his last speech of every campaign in Bedford. Previously the speeches had been held at the high school gymnasium to near-capacity crowds. By 1958, though, people no longer looked at speeches as entertainment in the evening; television had replaced politics. Instead of crowds of two or three thousand, only 700 were there for this final campaign speech. Subsequently, good oratorical skills were not nearly as necessary for a political career. Vance Hartke succeeded Jenner; neither Hartke nor Otis Bowen could boast of outstanding oratorical skills. It is also true that Jenner's oratorical style may not have been compatible with television.

Jenner gave his farewell speech on the U.S. Senate floor on August 21, 1958 (Congressional Record, Senate). He noted that he first came to the United States Senate in 1944. At that time the United States was at the summit of American power. America was the moral leader of the world. "We were fortified socially by the conviction that we had never used our superior power to impose our will on any other people. We expected nothing from our sacrifices except liberty for all nations, and the peace that goes with freedom," he stated. Jenner asked, "What has happened to that America?" He then went on to list the dangers and changes to America:

1. "efforts by a little group of willful men to perpetuate … unrestrained executive power …";

2. the replacement of the principles of the Atlantic Charter which promised self-determination by agreements at Tehran, Yalta and Potsdam; and

3. the subversion of American ideas of free enterprise in foreign trade "by GATT and … the blueprint for one economic world."

He argued that a Soviet Union that had been so weak in 1944 that it barely survived Hitler now controlled almost half the earth. However, the people knew that communism was death, and they were fleeing communism for the free world in Germany and Yugoslavia. In Korea refugees were clinging by the hundreds to every truck leaving North Korea for the South, and Chinese were fleeing from the mainland in junks to Taiwan.

Jenner declared, "Our people have not failed. Our principles have not been found wanting. Our political leaders have failed … It is the task of political operatives … to mediate among the many special interests and to find answers that serve the common good … The duty of our party is to serve … the interest of those Americans who ask no gifts from their country, who believe … that the government does not support the people. The people support their government." This was three years before Kennedy's famous inaugural speech in 1961 where he said, "Ask not what your country can do for you, but ask what you can do for your country."

After stating his opposition to world government and the perversion of the treaty power, Jenner concluded, "Firstly I have fought … against the weakening of America through financial waste … extravagance, red-ink budgets, the lies about owing our debt to ourselves …." He continued, "The founders of our country understood how essential it is to keep government close to poverty's edge. They put the control over expenditures into the hand of congress for a single reason. The congress whenever it appropriated the money would not have the spending of it … The executive … was not permitted to appropriate it, or lay taxes to collect it." Ultimately, Jenner said, "A government with too much money to spend destroys the society it governs …."

Several senators spoke on the floor immediately after the speech. Senator Jacobs Javits of New York said, "notwithstanding our disagreements on many fundamental matters of policy, I appreciate the sincerity, and respect, the indefatigable energy and erudition, with which he has attacked problems in his way, as I have tried to do in my own. I believe in this way each of us makes his contribution to what is good for the United States and the free world." Senator John Sherman Cooper of Kentucky said that Jenner was "relentless in his views" but "tolerant of the views of others. I know that he is a man who deeply loves his country … I know he is an American of great patriotism and of strong convictions."

Senator Prescott Bush stated that Jenner's service on the Senate finance committee had been invaluable, and his replacement would be difficult to find. Senator Estes Kefauver praised his service on the judiciary committee and said that "he has always been a man of his word" and "there could not be a more likable or charming person to work with on a committee or in the senate."

Much of 1958, with Jenner completing his last year in the Senate, was taken up with the efforts to secure passage of the Jenner-Butler bill, co-sponsored by Senator John M. Butler, a Democrat from Maryland. The bill was based on the power of Congress to limit the appellate jurisdiction of the U.S. Supreme Court. The founders, as part of the separation of powers concept, had clearly provided for such congressional action. The United States Constitution states in Article III, Section 2, Clause 2 as follows: "the Supreme Court shall have appellate jurisdiction … under such exceptions and under such regulations as the Congress shall make."

In ten decisions in 18 months, the Supreme Court had nullified all state laws against subversive efforts to overthrow the government on the premise that the Smith Act had "pre-exempted" that field. (No less than 59 anti-communist prosecutions had to be dismissed because of these decisions.) The bill would have removed the jurisdiction of the Supreme Court to overrule state bar examination boards regarding the qualifications of attorneys and allow states to enforce their own anti-subversive laws. After extensive hearings presided over by Jenner, the judiciary committee approved the measure on May 1, 1958, by a vote of ten to five. The bill was defeated on the Senate floor by a vote of 49 to 41.

In 1958 Federal Budget Director Maurice H. Stans estimated that the year's fiscal budget would produce a deficit of $12.2 billion and raise the federal debt to $283 billion by the next June 30. Jenner opposed increasing the debt ceiling to accommodate this, saying that the solution to constantly increasing government debt was to refuse to raise the debt ceiling.

Jenner also took parting shots at federal aid to education. "The American people are being brain-washed to accept multi-billion dollar appropriations for educational projects, and the scientific school bill is just a case of federal aid to education advocates using the Sputnicks to spin a fast one. Education requires more homework than money," he declared.

As Jenner was leaving the Senate, Lou Hiner on August 20 in the *News* summarized and described his philosophy as "anchored to the United States Constitution" which "offers clearly defined rights of every man...." The article described him as a "spokesman for State's rights ... a fighter against the one-world theory and an outspoken foe of concentrated power in a bureaucracy. The 'Marengo Kid' feels that opponents of the constitution are trying to destroy us from within by financial ruin ... No other man in the senate's membership can match a Jenner speech. His is the old-style oratory. The rising voice, the clinched [sic] fist, the rising up on the toes to make a point. That's Jenner. No one else can do it."

Hiner knew Jenner's personality and persuasions well, as he was the well-respected Washington correspondent for the *News*. These correspondents had become wondering admirers of the man they were covering, trying to separate their own views on politics from respect for this affable, strong-principled public servant; they were saying goodbye to one of the best story-makers they had come upon in their career as working journalists. For the Hiner article, Jenner reminisced that he had first come to Washington as an elevator boy in 1926, a job that Congressman Jimmy Dunbar of New Albany had found for him. The job paid $4.00 a day. Now years later he was looking forward to retirement, and on his return home he was going to take his son, "Billy and his gang," on a fishing weekend at the cabin on White River. He concluded in this article, "I have no regrets ... I've said and I've done what I honestly believe in. I will stand on the basic principles I came here with in 1944."

Jenner had earlier set the groundwork for his opinion as he had outlined his stand against aid to Russian satellite countries in a statement on March 3, 1958, on the issue of a $98 million grant to Poland (Congressional Record, Senate, March 3, 1958): "The satellite nations are the arsenals which maintain the Soviet war machine. Their unwilling people are enslaved to provide the food, the oil, the uranium, and the armament the Soviet Union must have to keep its war machine in high gear." He continued, "[T]he Soviet economy is inherently wasteful. The cost of party Commissars, purges, occupation troops and economic espionage is so high that the Soviet Union must make up for its inefficiency by tribute from its neighbors in a twentieth century revival of human slavery … When the Soviet rulers are once again limited to Soviet food production … oil … and war materials … the bold policies of the Soviet leaders will be less bold…" He declared that the grant was openly defended on the ground that it would pacify Polish farmers who were angry at Soviet forcible grain collection: "Thus it is proposed that Americans help quiet the patriotic resistance of the Polish farmers to Soviet exploitation." Jenner concluded that our self-interest and "and highest moral principles should lead to a policy of blocking Soviet exploitation of its satellite nations and preventing the enslavement of millions of human beings." The prophetic voice of these statements and knowledge of subsequent events gives us pause today.

On August 20, 1958, Senator William Revercomb of West Virginia put into the Congressional Record that in the retirement of Jenner, "we lose the service of a courageous patriot and statesman. However much others may differ with him, they know he fights for those principles he believes to be right." On the same date, Senator Alexander Wiley of Wisconsin said that in all things, Jenner was a sincere, earnest battler for his views. Wiley also noted, "working with him as I have on the Senate Judiciary Committee … he is a conscientious worker who fights hard for the right, as he sees it."

At a July 10, 1958, testimonial dinner, Senator William Knowland, Republican of California and senate minority leader, quoted Jenner's administrative assistant, Nyles Jackson, regarding the real reason for Jenner's retirement. Why would he retire at age 49, 26th in seniority in the Senate and 11th among Republicans? When Knowland pressed Jackson for an answer, Jackson said Jenner told him:

"Well, Nyles, as you know, I was born in Marengo, Indiana. When I go back there and walk down the street I know every person I meet. I went to school with most of them. I know their children. They are my friends. I have a sense of belonging to the community. It's my home town.

"You know my boy Billy has never had a home town. He has never had a chance to settle down in one place, go to school, make his friends, and have a feeling of belonging. We have jerked him back and forth across the country, had him in different schools, and lived in different houses trying to keep up with the changing political scene. He is now 15 and is a freshman in high school. We are only going to have him home with us about three more years and then he will be away at college. If Janet and I are ever going to be able to give him a real home like I had and let him grow up in a community where he can have his friends, where there are people who he really cares about and where the people really care about him, we are going to have to provide it for him in the next few years. He's got a right to these things, and in the business of politics, I haven't had a chance to give them to him. During the next three years his mother and I want him to be able to sink his roots into something that he can call home. I want him to be able to feel safe and secure and cared for in his own home town and community. You cannot develop those things in Washington. At least I cannot do so. Back in Indiana I can. I guess that's the real reason. At least, that's the best way I can put it."

Knowland concluded by saying, "In these days when the problems of juvenile delinquency are so acute, and parental evasion of family responsibilities so frequent, it is heartwarming to see a man think and act in terms of deep obligations to his family and home community. This is part of the basic Americanism we have come to associate with Bill Jenner."

Jenner had announced his decision to retire from the Senate in December of 1957 at the zenith of his power in Indiana politics and on the heels of triumphs over the Craig forces and the *Washington Post* on December 3 reported, "Jenner Remains Tops in Politics of Indiana." The paper speculated that he would run for governor in 1960. It was also thought that he felt alone, especially after the deaths of Joe McCarthy and of Senator Herman Welker, Republican of Idaho and a close friend.

Bill Jenner was not as alone as one might think. More than 1,200 people attended the testimonial dinner, which was held at the Sheraton Park Hotel in Washington, DC. Included among the guests were 16 U.S. senators with whom he was serving. These included Bridges of New Hampshire, Bricker of Ohio, Byrd of Virginia, Dirksen of Illinois, Goldwater of Arizona, Knowland of California, Malone of Nevada, McClelland of Arkansas, Mundt of South Dakota and John Williams of Delaware. Also there were prominent Indiana Democrats Frank M. McHale and Frank E. McKinney, as well as Indiana federal judges Robert Grant, Cale J. Holder and Democrat William E. Steckler.

At the farewell dinner it was remembered that Jenner suffered damage to his vision in World War II and "he hasn't been able to see Europe since." At the conclusion of the evening, Dad, Mom and I stood on the stairs and shook hands with all who came, and then turned our thoughts towards home.

Times photo by Raymond D. Brigl

GOP SPECIAL EDITION—Matching notes on the upcoming state and national election are (left to right) U. S. Sen. William Jenner, Rep Charles Halleck and Republican Nation. Committeeman Ralph Gates as they dined last night with the Indiana Republican Editori. Association.

A son is still a man's best friend, though we both loved our dog Kelly. Here we are listening to election returns on the radio, 1952.

1952, gubernatorial and senatorial candidates and their wives. (l to r) George Craig and his wife Kathryn; Janet and Bill Jenner.

Ike with the Indiana congressional delegation, 1952. Dad is holding the attention of President Eisenhower, who was sometimes amused by the Indiana senator.

President Dwight D. Eisenhower poses (in the middle) with the Republican senators in 1953. Nixon is second from left in front row; Homer Capehart at far right. Dad is behind and left of Ike. Robert Taft is second from left, back row. Taft died later that year.

They're Off For The GOP Derby!

1956 convention from the Indianapolis Star. *Cartoon by Pulitzer Prize winning cartoonist Charles Werner.*

Richard Nixon was not a close friend of Dad's but instead a political colleague during certain years. This is 1957. Also here are (l) Marion County Republican Chairman Dale Brown and (r) Robert Matthews, Republican state chairman.

Dad was always being interviewed. Here with Harold Handley, probably 1957.

Senator Jenner Faces Press Over Hoosier Fried Chicken

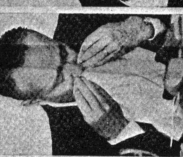

—The News Photos, Robert Lavelle

SENATOR WILLIAM E. JENNER . . . back on the Hoosier fried chicken circuit

. . . Unsound fiscal policies are taking too big a bite of the taxpayers' dollars

. . . Hoosier politicians always run until they die or are defeated

. . . In a major political party we don't all have to be Mikes, Ikes, look-alikes

. . . It's good to be back in Indiana after four years of "exile." (Story on Page

Dad is getting ready to possibly be escorted by a Pinkerton convention guard out of the 1960 National Republican convention for carrying and waving a Goldwater sign. Matthews is with him.

(l to r) State Republican Chairman Robert Matthews, Republican National Committeewoman Ione Harrington and her husband, Mom, Dad, and lifelong friends Kate and Frank "Bus" Pope.

Family games and reading were an important part of my upbringing. Friday night was movie night when we lived in Washington. That teddy bear seemed to go everywhere with me.

I always liked it when Dad talked about his 1949 congressional trip abroad. He is riding a camel in Egypt.

Janet and Bill were always hams at heart. Here they are singing and dancing in our backyard in Washington, DC.

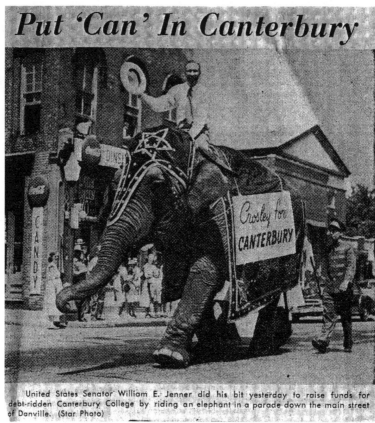

Put 'Can' In Canterbury

United States Senator William E. Jenner did his bit yesterday to raise funds for debt-ridden Canterbury College by riding an elephant in a parade down the main street of Danville. (Star Photo)

Bill Jenner had completed high school credits at Central Normal College in 1925. Now as Canterbury College, it was experiencing financial troubles.

Here Eisenhower is NOT recoiling from Bill Jenner on his left, as he campaigns. Charlie Halleck is at right and there's half a face of George Craig behind President Eisenhower. Butler University, September 10, 1952.

XVIII

POLITICS AFTER RETIREMENT

Bill Jenner's retirement was not uneventful.

On May 8, 1959, the IU Republican Club presented a portrait of Jenner to the Indiana University Law School, from which he had graduated in 1932. It was to be accepted in a ceremony that would include local and state dignitaries.

IU Law School Dean Leon H. Wallace gave the welcoming speech, and the portrait was officially accepted by Willis Hickam of the IU Board of Trustees. University President Herman Wells presided over the ceremony, which included an address by Governor Harold W. Handley. The portrait was placed on a wall with those of presidential candidate Wendell Willkie, former Dean and Indiana Governor Paul V. McNutt, Congressman Charles Halleck and former Supreme Court Justice Sherman Minton. Jenner and Minton were at that time the only IU law graduates who had been elected to the U.S. Senate.

The unveiling was picketed by ten students protesting Jenner's conservative stances. Jenner smilingly upheld the students' right to protest, noting that only totalitarian governments such as that of Russia demand conformity, and that America stands for "freedom of individuals and freedom of thought." The *Bloomington Herald Telephone* editorial page called the contest the next day: "Jenner the Winner After Picket Parade." President Wells later issued a statement rebuking the pickets for "a regrettable display of bad manners" and stated that he wished every student could have heard Senator Jenner's statement in defense of minority views. "It was a classic statement of fundamental American doctrine, to which we all subscribe …."

Jenner was elected at the 1960 Indiana Republican convention as a delegate-at-large to the Republican national convention. Eisenhower's vice-president, Richard Nixon, was the odds-on favorite to win the presidential nomination. However, it was reported that Jenner was ready to swing the Indiana delegation to U.S. senator Barry Goldwater "if Barry says the word." Jenner and many other conservatives were angered when Nixon met with Governor Nelson Rockefeller of New York and accepted his demands to alter the Republican platform.

While Eisenhower, at a convention breakfast in Chicago, was urging Republican candidates to follow "the great middle road," Jenner was enlivening the caucus of the Indiana delegates by shouting "to Hell with the Republican platform." "We'll run on a statement of principles like Judd's [keynoter Representative Walter Judd of Minnesota] and we'll win." Jenner said he was sick and tired of the Republican Party "trying to outbid the damn New Dealers!"

On Monday night at the convention, Goldwater made a speech that touched off a spontaneous demonstration involving many of the delegates. Jenner grabbed the Indiana standard and pumped it up and down as he took part in the parade through the aisles.

Of the platform concessions, Jenner declared that the people were being disenfranchised by a lack of anything to choose from, "like Tweedledum and Tweedledee," the *Bedford Daily Times Mail* reporter wrote on July 25, 1960.

A 1959 editorial noted that while still in office Jenner spoke to a group of newspaper publishers from many states. Many, because of what they heard of Jenner, considered skipping the luncheon. However, most attended and "almost to a man" they "left praising Mr. Jenner" for his honesty.

He did fulfill his promise to my mother and me to give us a great deal of attention. With Dad retired, my college education was much more secure. I attended Indiana University in Bloomington, 23 miles north of our home in Bedford. I graduated in 1966 with a BA and an LLB law degree. I worked two years as a law clerk for United States District Court Judge Cale J. Holder. I was able to secure this position rather easily due to Holder's long friendship with my father. I moved to Madison, Indiana, in 1968, opened a private law practice and served as deputy prosecutor for Harold E. Ford.

As for Mother, after Dad's retirement, she became active as a founder and member of the Bedford Little Theatre. She acted in many plays and directed many more. Dad called her "the Director." However, he was very proud of her ability and was quite content to take a back seat to her interest in theater. In retirement he enjoyed farming, and together they had great fun with a small houseboat on Lake Monroe near Bloomington. All in all they seemed to have a very happy and successful marriage, and I know my Dad admired her very much. When we were in the car I can remember them singing and harmonizing together on songs such as "Way Back When," "You Made Me Love You" and "You Must Have Been a Beautiful Baby."

Dad paid less and less attention to politics as the years went on. In 1966 he actively backed John R. Snyder's successful campaign for state treasurer. He also served with Harold Handley, Homer Capehart and Ralph Gates on the 1964 platform committee for the Indiana Republican convention. He was a delegate to the 1976 Republican national convention in Kansas City, where Gerald Ford was nominated to seek the presidency against Georgia Governor Jimmy Carter.

He served as Indiana state chairman for Ronald Reagan's successful 1980 bid for the Republican presidential nomination. That job was mainly honorary, as he was in failing health by that time, suffering from increasing difficulty with his sight and arthritis. He lived to see the election of Ronald Reagan as president. He was surprised by the result and harbored a faint hope that, as he had previously thought Taft's election would accomplish, this could be the end of monolithic executive and national power as well as deficit spending. However, Reagan's administration proved to be only a temporary pause in what Jenner claimed to be a deplorable trend.

Rumors continued for years that Jenner would run for governor. Asked at the 1964 Republican state convention if he would consider a gubernatorial draft, he replied, "Why, if they did that and offered me a baby's potty, made of gold, rimmed with rubies and emeralds and filled with diamonds, I'd be forced to tell them where they should put it." So the *Star* said on June 10 of that year.

On Kennedy's death in 1963, Jenner was quoted as saying, "my heartfelt sympathy goes to his family ... I served for six years with the late President in the Senate. While we might have disagreed politically we were still close personal friends."

XIX

SPEAKING STYLE

Dad's speaking style has been described in various ways. James Madison in *The Indiana Way: A State History* said that "his salty language and gift for political invective seldom have been matched in Indiana politics." William D. Pickett, in *Homer E. Capehart: A Senator's Life 1897–1979*, described Dad as, "Slender and handsome, Jenner ... considered Washington an alien place ... an abundance of energy and a sharp tongued humor made him a formidable orator. He frequently combined a warm smile with recrimination. His strident but earthy style attracted supporters."

Madison, in *Indiana Through Tradition and Change: A History of the Hoosier State and Its People*, noted that in 1936, "William E. Jenner, a young State senator from Paoli, made one of the liveliest speeches in twentieth century Indiana politics; with humor, sarcasm and biting criticism, Jenner lambasted 'Paul the Fifth' [McNutt] as the 'flaxen haired beauty of Bloomington.'" Madison also noted that "Jenner was an effective campaigner—able to draw on small town origins, spellbind a crowd—talented—young and aggressive."

He was also quick on his feet. An older gentleman in Madison told my son Joe that he had attended a Jenner rally as a young man in the late thirties or early forties. Someone yelled from the audience, "Is Janet pregnant?" Jenner looked at the man and said, "I can't answer that, but I can tell you she's been exposed."

It was reported that long after his retirement he could still "steal the show" at Republican functions. Governor Bowen and Senator Richard Lugar would give "good talks," but it was reported that their applause paled in comparison with the applause given to Jenner.

Clarence Manion, former dean of the Notre Dame Law School,

told David Tudor for his series of interviews that he remembered a speech Dad had given in the legislature in opposition to the WPA and the outdoor privies that Eleanor Roosevelt had the WPA building. (We have one of them at the cabin.) Jenner made a speech to the glory of the privy and had "everybody literally rolling in the aisles."

Frank Millis, who served in the state legislature and also terms as auditor of state and state treasurer, had been Dad's campaign manager in his 1940 campaign for governor. (Later Millis teamed with Craig in an attempt to deny Handley the gubernatorial nomination in 1956.) He said that he and Dad drove 60,000 miles over the state by car prior to the 1940 convention. They "wore out two Fords." He said to the Tudor series interviewers that Jenner could "get up and make a rip roaring speech, and he's the fastest thinker on his feet of anybody I know … He's got a trigger mind, and he's just a brilliant orator." Clark Springer in the same interview series said, "Jenner was of the old school of oratory … he could hold an audience right in the palm of his hand."

He had developed his style over many years, and it went a long way back. His first speech was at a Crawford County patriotic event on the Fourth of July. The organizers asked his father, Woody Jenner, if his son would give a speech. Young Jenner was home from college and told his dad that he was no speech maker, to which his father replied, "Goddamn, son, you've been to college: surely you can give a goddamn speech." He gave the speech and from all accounts seemed to be a natural orator. As a young man, I observed his speeches. He would shout, but then he would whisper. He would make the audience laugh and then make them cry. By the conclusion of a speech, I believe they would have marched on the courthouse if he had asked them.

I remember being aware of him on a campaign in 1952. Television ads were practically non-existent, and radio and newspaper ads were also not utilized much in these days before political action committees with huge funding efforts. His campaign consisted of an old Ford station wagon with a loudspeaker attached to the roof. He and his campaign manager would go to a town and ride through it during the day, announcing through the loudspeaker that Senator Jenner would be speaking at a place in the community that evening.

The one thing I really remember was what a physical thing a speech was for him. About halfway through, he would usually take off his coat and throw it behind him, which always brought a cheer from the crowd. This was not, however, a merely theatrical flourish, because he had worked up a sweat with his orating. When he left the stage after a speech, he was ringing wet with sweat. His campaign manager or assistant always had a clean, dry shirt for him to put on after a speech because his other shirt was literally soaking.

Irving Leibowitz had editorialized in the *Times* that nobody who had heard Jenner speak "will ever forget his palm slapping, feet stomping, finger wagging way of oratory ... He rang the rafters with his blood and thunder political speeches in the Billy Sunday style." His speaking ability made him a frequent and able debater on the U.S. Senate floor—often called the greatest debating society in the world.

It is interesting to read his extemporaneous remarks on the floor of the Senate during this time. For example, on February 28, 1947, he chastised Democrats for their inability to reduce the debt or taxes:

"If we are going to reduce the debt and taxes, ... the way to do it is by reducing the expenditures and ... by efficiency in government" (Congressional Record, Senate, February 28, 1947).

"Indiana's ... share of foreign-aid cost would pay for maintaining Indiana's public schools for a period of more than eleven years at the 1946–1947 level of school expenditures ..." (Congressional Record, Senate, January 28, 1948).

"I say that the only chance for Russian domination of the world is the failure of America and the failure of the free-enterprise systems" (Congressional Record, Senate, March 13, 1948).

"[S]ome may call me an isolationist ... some may call me a reactionary, and some may call me a conservative ... but I say to you that I stand here today as a liberal, because one who will preserve his country ... and its freedoms and will give liberty and justice to our people is the greatest liberal there can be" (Congressional Record, Senate, January 18, 1949).

On civil rights Jenner argued with Senator Claude Pepper of Florida that "President Roosevelt had an overwhelming majority for 16 years ... and the same civil rights, about which the senator from Florida yells so loudly today, were being denied the same 16,000,000 people during those same 16 years, but nothing was done about it. Furthermore the present President of the United States [Truman] was a member of the august body; and … I can find no determined effort that he made for 10 years as a senator from Missouri to lead the fight for civil rights."

Finally, after Pepper had complained of Republicans previously supporting cloture (allowing for filibuster), Dad asserted, "Mr. President, I am sure the senator knows that consistency is a jewel. I now hold in my hand a Record of the United States Senate of January 27, 1938 … to close debate on the … anti-lynch bill, and I find there were 51 votes … against the cloture petition and there were only 12 Republicans among the 51 names. But the startling thing is that I find — … that the senator from Florida [Mr. Pepper] voted against cloture in 1938 on the anti-lynching bill. Consistency, thou art a jewel" (Congressional Record, Senate, March 17, 1949).

In another debate with Senator Pepper regarding the Depression, Jenner argued:

Mr. Jenner: Is it not a fact that the senator loves the common man, the poor man of America so much, that he does not want to give him even a 30 percent reduction in his taxes?

Mr. Pepper: Yes; but I want to be judged by my love for the poor man and not by my love for the rich man.

Mr. Jenner: The Democrats had 14 years to demonstrate their love for the poor man, and nothing has been done about it.

Mr. Pepper: And there were 20,000,000 persons unemployed.

Mr. Jenner: … is the senator saying that there were 20,000,000 unemployed in Mr. Hoover's time?

Mr. Pepper: That is right.

Mr. Jenner: According to that, all of us were selling apples to each other. [laughter] (Congressional Record, Senate, March 31, 1947).

The Bureau of Labor Statistics has estimated that 12,830,000 persons were unemployed in 1933 at the peak of the Depression.

Dad was very committed to the concept that the United States was a republic, not a democracy: "Mr. President, we are not a democracy. We never were intended to be a democracy. This nation is a republic and there is no reference in the preamble, in the constitution, in any of the debates at the convention which framed the constitution, or in any of the sacred documents of this great nation, which calls us a democracy. But we are fast getting to be a democracy, because we are becoming a government of organized gangs."

Jenner cited a pamphlet of the Americans for Democratic Action in 1949 affirming that British planning and social welfare was proceeding without losing democratic practices. Jenner scoffed: "They have lost their freedoms over there. My wife was born in that country. I know ... first hand ... that if a man is a coal miner and wants to quit his job and go into some other industry, he cannot do so without receiving permission. He must go to the bureaucrats to receive permission."

Senator Hubert Humphrey (at that time president of Americans for Democratic Action) rejoined: "Did I understand you to say that democracy was nothing more or less than an organization of gangs?"

Mr. Jenner: I said the type of government we are getting in this country is organized gang rule. If you have the biggest gang, if you wield the biggest political club, you are going to have the biggest power .... They do not care what happens to America. It is time somebody stood on the floor of the Senate ... and stood for America regardless of his political future. What will anybody's political future amount to ... if we lose our liberty? ... (Congressional Record, Senate, April 7, 1949).

Holmes Alexander, the respected syndicated columnist, in 1957 pegged Jenner as the one speaker in the Senate no tourist would want to miss—a Senate that incuded Everett Dirksen and John F. Kennedy.

Lou Hiner, Jr. of the *News* wrote on August 20, 1958: "No other man in the Senate's present membership can match a Jenner speech. His is the old style oratory. The rising voice, the clinched [sic] fist, the rising up on the toes to make a point. That's Jenner. No one else can do it."

XX

THE HUMOR OF BILL JENNER

I don't know if my dad was truly funny, but he was entertaining, and people seemed to enjoy his company. My mother used to say that if he went in a doctor's office waiting room and there were two or more patients, he would strike up a conversation and entertain the waiting people. I always thought had he not been in politics, he could have been a successful actor or singer.

Nyles Jackson remarked when being interviewed by David Tudor about something I have heard others say. "He really should have been on the stage …. If he walked into this room, two of us or two hundred of us, all eyes would be on him in a couple of minutes …. He had a great ability to just take over the situation."

Jackson also remembered that in a bad situation, Jenner would say, "Forget it. When the cats pissed in the milk, there's no use to strain it." In a similar vein, if a situation was hopeless, he would say, "that ball belongs to Joe Hays"—an old saying his mother used to use. If a colleague would not stand firm on an issue, Jenner would say, "anybody's dog can hunt with him." If a politician seemed confused, Jenner would compare him to the "boy who dropped his bubble gum in the hen house."

He was quoted in the *Chicago Tribune* on August 11, 1968, at the Republican national convention where Nixon was nominated as realizing that he was not always popular among his colleagues. He told the assembled reporters that while he was making the Marshall speech, he felt a twinge in his chest. Without halting his denunciation of Marshall, he said to himself, "Oh Lord, don't take me now; I haven't got enough friends on the floor to carry me off."

Politically he had a way of characterizing people in novel but descriptive ways. His reference to Indiana Governor Paul V. McNutt, the "flaxen-haired beauty from Bloomington," has been quoted before. Jenner's political views didn't carry any real animosity; he attended McNutt's funeral. He characterized Joe McCarthy, who was initially embraced by the liberal press because of his progressive domestic views, as being like "the little boy who was invited to the birthday party and pissed in the lemonade." Dad contended the establishment only turned on McCarthy after he started investigating communists.

Richard Nixon said on national television that Jenner said that Secretary of State Averell Harriman was "thin as piss on a rock." Dad meant that Harriman was weak and carried little weight. (Apparently Dad was not alone in this view. Arthur M. Schlesinger, Jr. says in his book *Robert Kennedy and His Times* that after an evening with Lord Beaverbrook in 1958, Robert Kennedy recorded that Beaverbrook said of Harriman, "Never has anyone gone so far with so little.") Dad later claimed that Nixon had misquoted him. He had actually called Harriman "thin as piss on a board"—not on a rock.

His stories often carried a political moral. When he was state chairman he was able to secure for his good friend, fishing and hunting buddy Doc Diefendorf, the position as executive secretary of the Indiana Alcoholic Beverage Commission. Doc Diefendorf was a retired dentist, a fine gentleman who lived in Mitchell, Indiana, in Lawrence County, the same county in which my parents and I resided.

Around Christmas Dad got a call at his office in Indianapolis. Doc said, "Bill, are you going home to Bedford this weekend?" When Dad replied affirmatively, Doc said, "Would you mind coming by my office on Friday afternoon? I've been given so much liquor for Christmas that I can't get it all in my car. Would you load some in your car and help me unload it at my house in Mitchell?" Dad went by the ABC office on Friday, and sure enough, it required both cars to load the whiskey. While they were unloading the whiskey at Doc's home in Mitchell, Dad said, "Now Doc, don't get used to this. Politics may change and this will end." Doc still insisted, "No, Bill, this has nothing to do with politics. These liquor distributors know and appreciate what a good job I'm doing and have made these gifts because they truly like and respect me."

Later politics did change and Doc lost his job with the ABC. Governor Gates fired him in 1948 for supporting Jenner's bid for governor. At Christmas Dad and his good friend Hugh Gray from Loogootee went by to see Doc at his home in Mitchell, taking with them a pint of Heaven Hill whiskey. Dad asked him how much liquor he had received as presents from the wholesalers who had been so generous the year before. Doc replied, "Not one god-damned bottle," whereupon Dad and Hugh gave him the pint of bourbon and said, "Merry Christmas, Doc. Your old friends didn't forget you."

While Dad was state chairman in 1945 he also had a small law office in Bedford. He was in need of a secretary and saw an employment ad from a Wilma Wood who lived in Lawrence County. She had experience after working in an office in Cincinnati, Ohio, for a couple of years, but had come home and needed a job in the Bedford area.

When Wilma first worked for my Dad, she got a call from Hugh Gray. Hugh was a great kidder with a dry sense of humor, so he did not give her his true name. When Wilma told him that Dad was not in, he told her to tell him, "Chief Wahoo of the Haw Creek Indian tribe called." Wilma, not knowing Hugh at the time, carefully transcribed the note and gave it to Dad when he returned to the office. Dad, of course, knew exactly who had made the call and got a great laugh.

Wilma Wood went on to become his secretary during his terms in the United States Senate, and when he retired she worked in his Indianapolis law office. Later she kept his books and correspondence when he completely retired to Bedford, Indiana. She was a true friend of our family, and after Dad's death she kept books and did correspondence for my mother. They were also great friends and played gin rummy and checked on each other by phone on a daily basis. When we were in Washington she would even babysit me if my parents were to be gone for more than a day.

Wilma was like a second mother to me, and I loved her very much. She and her boyfriend, Nelson Deranian, would take me with them to eat when she would "sit" with me. (I remember a really great Italian restaurant, but I can't recall the name. The other restaurant was Arbaugh's that had great ribs, fried chicken and onion rings. I am sure both restaurants are gone now.) Nelson was originally from Indianapolis and was a very successful attorney in Washington, DC, mainly representing "dime stores." She and Nelson never married (he had an elderly mother whom he cared for), but they corresponded until his death. Wilma had one of the greatest dispositions I have ever seen. She was always cheery and full of laughs and fun. My wife says she was that way because she never married.

Wilma told me that Dad, whom she didn't know at the time, called her in response to her ad. His only question was, "Do you have female trouble?" Somewhat taken aback by the question, she replied that she did not. Thereupon he advised her that she was hired and to report to work on Monday. Later when she would tell the story, Dad would respond, "Yes, and that's the last god-damned time I'll ever hire a secretary sight unseen over the telephone," to which Wilma would reply, "Yes, and that's the last time I'll ever accept a job offered over the phone."

One of my favorite stories occurred at our cabin at Shoals. Dad was in his late seventies and couldn't hunt, but he was looking forward to eating some pheasant that we had killed earlier in Nebraska. I had gone hunting earlier in the day, and at the first shot my gun-shy bird dog Katy had run back to the truck.

In cooking the pheasant, we turned the heat to high and scorched the pheasant meat. The end result was practically inedible. After dinner Dad yelled at me, "Billy, go out and bring Katy in here." I said, "Dad, why do you want that gun-shy dog in here?" He replied, "Because I want to kiss her ass and get this bad taste out of my mouth."

He enjoyed the humor of others. He used to go to the racetrack at Churchill Downs, and one day went with Frank McHale, a prominent, influential and wealthy Democrat. McHale was a bachelor and had no children. Dad noticed that he was a heavy bettor, wagering $500 to $1,000 a race. Dad therefore would follow him to the betting window and place lesser bets on the same horses that McHale was betting. At the end of the day someone asked McHale how he had done, and McHale replied that he had a successful and great day. Dad said, "You lying son of a bitch. I bet every horse you did and never cashed a ticket." McHale said, "Bill, you don't understand. I had a great day. Only my heirs and devisees had a bad day."

At the age of 72 Dad was again a delegate to the Republican national convention in Detroit in 1980. He recalled the first national convention he attended in 1928 with his father in Kansas City. The Indiana delegation, led by Senator James Watson, had joined some other states in an effort to block Herbert Hoover's nomination. (Hoover was actually considered to be from the liberal wing of the GOP.) However, when

Pennsylvania went for Hoover, the stampede for him was on. Almost all the delegations, except Indiana, got up and joined a victory parade on the floor. (This was similar to Indiana's reaction at the 1952 convention.) Jenner said, "I was way up in the top balcony. A big guy sitting next to me said, 'Who is that bunch of bastards down there that won't join in?' I took my Indiana badge off and put it in my pocket 'cause hell, I was afraid he was going to throw me over the balcony" (*Louisville Courier Journal*, July 13, 1980). In the same interview he correctly predicted that Reagan would win the presidency that year over Jimmy Carter.

On September 23, 1950, Jenner attacked columnist Drew Pearson on the floor of the Senate (Congressional Record, Senate, September 23, 1950). He noted that Pearson had been called an SOB by two presidents of the United States. However, Jenner thought that such an attack was unfair, for it "thoughtlessly cast reflections on his family." Jenner said Pearson was not an SOB; he was a "self-appointed, self-made, cross T'd, dotted I'd, double documented, super superlative revolving S.O.B." Jenner concluded by calling Pearson a "propaganda peddling proselyte of the nation's press." Pearson had written an article accusing Al Beverage of being the ghostwriter for Jenner's recent speech on General Marshall. Jenner pointed out that his facts were wrong, and that Beverage had been dead for 18 months when Jenner made the speech.

Dad was very close to his older brother Donald Jenner, who stayed in Marengo and ran the general store and Ford agency under the name of W. E. Jenner and Sons. The store had continued on, with the Ford agency and a repair shop in the basement and in the upstairs hardware, furniture, linoleum, carpet, appliances and television sets. Dad would visit Donald often in Marengo when he was home from the Senate. As I've previously said, Dad was always home for the Fourth of July, as the Senate would recess in the summer and not reconvene until the following January. He spent six months at home talking to fellow Hoosiers and visiting his old haunts and relatives rather than speaking with lobbyists.

Dad told me the following story about the Margengo emporium his family ran:

A man accompanied by his wife and family came into the general store while my dad was there. They told Donald that they wanted to buy a TV, thereupon Donald, who had a gruff countenance, advised the family that the TVs were not good or well made and that they would be making a mistake in purchasing one.

After the couple and their children left the store, Dad said, "Hell, Donald, no wonder the store's not doing well. That's no way to sell anything." Donald replied, "Now Bill, you're over in Washington, and maybe you know what you're doing there, but you don't know the people here in Marengo any more. Those people can't afford a TV. If I sold it, they would be unable to make the payments, and I would have to repossess it. You've never had to repossess a TV from a home where the children are crying because you're taking their TV while they're watching 'Howdy Doody.' You go back to Washington, and let me take care of the store."

Marengo's water never passed the state test for purity. Therefore everyone drank impure water. Donald had a dry sense of humor. I remember him telling Dad on many occasions, "Well, Old So and So died." Dad would reply, "How old was he?" Donald would tell the deceased's age, usually in the late eighties or early nineties. Dad would then inquire as to what killed him. Donald would invariably reply, "Bad water."

One story a friend of mine attributed to my dad: Governor Handley, the former governor of Indiana (1956–1960), and Dad's friend, while vacationing in Wyoming in 1972 died of a heart attack at the age of 63. According to the story, a friend of Handley and Dad attended the funeral visitation. The friend, viewing Handley in the casket, exclaimed, "Doesn't Harold look good?" Whereupon Dad was reputed to say, "Hell, he ought to. He just got back from vacation." I do not know if this story is true, but it certainly sounds like something he might have said.

XXI

RETROSPECT

In retirement the former Senator Jenner was dividing his working time between his law practice in Indianapolis and his Orange County farm where he was raising Charolais cattle.

In a 1971 interview with Kristie Hill of the *Indiana Republican News*, he decried the fact that politicians were no longer willing to stand up for conservative principles: "The liberals haven't destroyed our country. It's the week-kneed sons of bitches who refuse to stand up for what they believed and who were only interested in getting re-elected."

In the same interview his secretary, Wilma Wood, was quoted as saying, "Sometimes people complained about his vocabulary, but you never had any trouble understanding what he was saying."

In the interview he also lamented that "We're committed now to deficit spending." Jenner was proud of the fact that he never lost a general election when he was in politics, including two elections to the Indiana Senate, a short-term election to the U.S. Senate, and the 1946 and 1952 elections to the U.S. Senate.

Still, at the close of his Senate career, he was realizing that his early hopes about change that would return America to its former leadership role had been largely in vain. He had trusted Republican Presidents and his own ideals and they had not been enough. "I went into politics thinking that when my party came into power it would all change. But it didn't. We just put a cloak of respectability on it. When Ike was president, we had a situation where you either liked Ike or you were a son-of-a-bitch. I wasn't here to like Ike; I was supposed to like my country."

BILL AND DONALD

A September 1975 article from the *Louisville Courier Journal* focused on the positive small town relationships among the Jenner clan. Dad Woody and the senator's two brothers, Loren and Donald Jenner, stayed close. This focus is on Bill and Donald.

"Crawford County's Lycarjus [sic] (Woody) Jenner was a self-made doer, a man who could have sold sand in the desert and left his buyers smiling. He sold the county's first cream separater [sic], first washing machine, first Ford, first gallon of gasoline. But more important he sold a way of life to his sons, Donald and Bill. Along with his wife, Jane, an orphan, he left his sons a legacy of free enterprise and contrary-minded individualism. They chose different routes through life—Donald deciding to stay at home to cuss the weather and the government while Bill went off to Washington to cuss the world. Today, from his law office in Indianapolis, Bill Jenner looks back and salutes his parents—'a mom who wanted me to go to college and a dad who didn't have any education but was as smart as an outhouse rat.' From his garage in Marengo, Donald Jenner bows in the same direction. 'Us Jenners give ulcers, we don't get 'em,' he says."

After Jenner's death, former governor George Craig was quoted as saying that although not always on the same side, they were "personal friends" since attending IU together in 1932. Craig said, "I always respected him. He was a great man, a dedicated patriotic American." Governor Robert Orr called him "a great public servant." He "favored military assistance to those countries ... fighting for independence ... and fought against control of ... military policy by certain foreign policy planners." He was remembered for warning against what he called dangerous "power elite" in the federal bureaucracy created by "big spending, the trend toward secrecy and the constitutional treaty clause." He was also noted for opposing the "Status of Forces," treaties whereby American soldiers could be arrested overseas and tried under the laws of the host country.

In March 1985, shortly before Jenner's death, *Indianapolis Star* writer Ben Cole said that the boisterous Jenner made living worth dying for. Cole recalled that Jenner had returned to Washington five months before for a Senate fundraising affair and had called Cole. Cole said in the article, "Covering Bill Jenner during his heyday was pure fun for any reporter—hectic, sometimes exasperating and exceedingly strenuous— but fun nevertheless." His nationalistic conservatism, Cole said, made him popular at home, but "repelled and outraged many liberal tilted correspondents ... It wasn't necessary to agree with his political views to have his friendship. When Matthew J. Connelly, President Truman's principal assistant was indicted for misconduct in office, Jenner appeared in court as one of his character witnesses ... He was always accessible to Indiana newsmen, quick with an apt comment and always delightfully quotable. When the Eisenhower administration espoused a farm price support program in the 50's, Jenner strode across the Capitol plaza, and in his own arm-waving ebullient way cried for all to hear, 'They'll be in office forever. They're going to give away money.' The summer of 1958 was a lonely time for Bill, with his family back in Indiana. One hot Monday morning he told me, 'You know what I did over the week end? I went to seven picture shows ... Jenner thought deeply about life's vicissitudes ... . He attended the funeral of Paul V. McNutt at Arlington National Cemetery ... As the casket was moved down the aisle, Jenner leaned over and said in a loud whisper, 'What's the use ... when we're all going to wind up that way anyway?' His embarrassed seatmate scribbled a note to him—'Bill, the idea is to make living worth dying for.' Days later that scrap of paper was taped to the desk lamp in Jenner's office. In his inexpressibly boisterous, individualistic way, Bill Jenner made living worth dying for."

News reporter Bill Roberts did a profile on April 30, 1976. Jenner, 68 at the time, was quoted as saying, "Most people think I'm dead by now, and some mornings I feel like I am."

On June 22, 1974, he and Senator Capehart were named honorary co-chairmen of the Indiana state Republican convention. When Jenner was presented with a miniature gavel, he said, "I appreciate the memento. I only wish I could hit a few Democrats in the head with it." A whole new generation of reporters like Roberts for the *Star* was covering and appreciating Bill Jenner.

Wilma Wood was his secretary from 1945 until his death. After his death she paid Janet's bills and kept in daily contact with her. She said Jenner "was a fiery, silver tongued orator and told it like it was." "They threw away the mold with Mr. Jenner," she told the *Bedford Times Mail* on August 7, 2001.

On the subject of the report "Interlocking Subversion in Government," the *Richmond Times Dispatch* editorialized, "Senator Jenner is not one of our favorite statesmen ... but it must be conceded that the report that he and his senate Subcommittee have unanimously made ... is one of the most startling documents of the decade ... All in all the Jenner subcommittee has done an effective and important piece of research."

Dad told the story of a recent return to the Senate chambers after more than 20 years' absence: "Former Senators are supposed to have lifetime access to the senate floor, but the guards there wouldn't let me in. I showed them my old senate pass with my photo on it ... taken when I was in my mid 30s, and I'm forty years older now and look like hell. They said they never heard of me.

"I was arguing with the sergeant-at-arms when Senator [John C.] Stennis of Mississippi, came along and explained who I am." As he entered the Senate chamber with Stennis, Dad turned to the guards, put his thumb to his nose and said, "Hey, you guys know how to spell pffffffffft?"

He also said in an interview with Tom Keating of the *Star*, "I've never missed Washington since I left. The last budget I voted on was $65 billion, and now it's what?—900 billion? I don't know what the hell is going on there anymore, and I wonder if the people there do either."

On the subject of Nixon, Jenner said in an interview given to Irving Leibowitz for the *Times* on July 8, 1973, that the president should have been impeached for stupidity: "There's not a politician among them. They had too much money and no political savvy." Jenner said that if Nixon had had a conversation with old pals like Goldwater, they might have undone the damage done by amateurs, but they couldn't get past the Palace Guard. The president was a virtual prisoner in the White House.

Jenner in one speech said that one good Indiana precinct committeeman could have helped Nixon more than the advisers he had. Jenner pointed out that the Republican Party was not involved in Watergate. There were no party officials involved. Jenner blamed Nixon's hand-picked technicians like John Ehrlichman, Bob Haldeman, John Dean, John Mitchell, Jeb Magruder and Charles Colson, men who were loyal to Nixon above party and country: "They never ran for political office, took a poll or worked in the precincts."

Jenner was described by the *Star*'s Washington Bureau Chief Ben Cole on January 2, 1983, as a flamboyant intellectual whose colleagues never knew what a brilliant, serious-minded senator he truly was. Cole wrote that he manifested a fiery conservatism ... with a zeal that frightened some of his fellow politicians. He considered himself an outsider."

The *Indianapolis Star* editorialized on March 12 of the year he died that he was "down to earth, lively, combative, a gifted orator who went unerringly to the heart of the matter. Senator Jenner gave a rare pungency and clarity to national debate. Indiana may not see his like again. If it doesn't, we will all be the losers."

XXII

PASSING OF THE TORCH

My father died on March 9, 1985, at the age of 76. He had suffered a massive stroke at his Bedford home earlier that week. Efforts to revive him at the Dunn Memorial Hospital in Bedford were unsuccessful. He had been afflicted with macular degeneration, progressive blindness and arthritis in his last several years. He was pleased that I had a wonderful wife, four sons and roots in the community of Madison, Indiana—roots he had worked hard for me to have. He also knew that as a result of his law practice after retirement, my mother was comfortable with no financial worries. My mother, Janet, assumed that she would pass shortly after his death, but she lived to be 93 and was a source of wisdom, strength and enjoyment to my family until her death in 2001.

On his death, Wilma Wood was quoted as saying, "Bill Jenner was a red-blooded fighting All American. He … devoted his public life to protecting what he deeply believed was good and in the best interest of his beloved state and country. He never sacrificed his principles and ideals to be on the popular side of issues" (Bedford *Times Mail*, March 11, 1985).

In a final summation, Irving Leibowitz described Jenner as a "rock-em, sock-em U.S. senator from Indiana." Jenner's critics branded him as a witch hunter, grand-stander, vigilante and grand inquisitor; his friends as a great patriot and a courageous battler against communism and subversion. He opposed foreign aid and cried that we were pouring money down rat holes, and that kind of heated rhetoric stirred up enemies.

Another opined that when Jenner was around "the air cackled with wit. His good humor was laced with the salt of earthy Hoosierisms. He fought dismantling German factories and shipping them to the Soviet Union as reparations. He denounced the 1954 accords in Geneva that divided Viet Nam and turned over 22 provinces to the Communists, saying with a prescience that was tragically accurate, that the accords had set Viet Nam up for the kill."

He persistently "railed against excessive spending ... warning ... that they were betraying their children and grandchildren with debt."

Perhaps the most incisive analysis came from an icon of conservative thought, Robert Novak.

Novak looks at Jenner's career.

Robert Novak, a nationally syndicated columnist and author of the "Evans-Novak Political Report," a political commentator for CNN, and member of the TV show "Cross Fire," remembers that as a young reporter he was assigned from the AP in Nebraska to the AP in Indiana.

"In 1955, three years had not healed the deep cleavage between the Indiana Republican party's Taft and Eisenhower wings." Novak states that he was influenced by a 1955 *Time* cover story on Governor George Craig, a former national commander of the American Legion—the article called him a "swift-footed, swashbuckling lawyer-politician." The magazine cast him as the great hope of Eisenhower's "New Republicans" aligned against the reactionary Taft wing headed by William Ezra Jenner.

Novak found things not nearly so simple. "The Indianapolis press corps despised Craig as a corrupt and arrogant bully. Jenner at least had some ideals, even if they were not as acceptable in the Republican party then as they would be a generation later. Limited government, low taxes, and 'home rule' (a euphemism for States' rights.)"

Novak observed that the Craig vs. Jenner showdown came during the party convention at the fairgrounds on June 29, 1956. Craig was booed by the party delegates chanting "We want Jenner." Handley, Jenner's choice, won—the only one of five candidates deemed unacceptable by Craig.

When Novak got to Washington, he found the

politicians generally uninspiring. "Then there was William E. Jenner of Indiana. When I got to know Jenner, I was surprised how easy it was to deal with a man described as unapproachable by my colleagues. Jenner was a genuine conservative who antagonized other members of the Indiana delegation by trying to limit pork for the state. In private conversations, he was intelligent and well informed."

Novak continued, "On December 2, 1957, Jenner announced he would not seek a third term. He was only forty-nine years old, at the height of his power as Indiana's dominant Republican. His retirement was unexpected, but ... no mystery for anybody who knew him. Jenner detested moderate Republicans and what he perceived as the nation's leftward drift at home and abroad, which he considered himself powerless to stop ...

Jenner thought himself the last of a defeated breed. He never dreamed Barry Goldwater would be nominated for president in six years and Ronald Reagan elected president sixteen years after that. Jenner was around for ... the Reagan Revolution but never saw it coming."

William Jenner's fight against communist internal subversion was successful. Enough light was thrown upon the subject that communist infiltration of our government has essentially ended. It died on the vine.

His views on civil rights have also prevailed. His position on dealing with Russia has also been proven—albeit much later—to be correct.

Was he right on the issues of executive power, foreign aid and one-world policy? Future historians will have to answer that.

He was, however, able to state his views with a clarity that is seldom approached by modern-day politicians. He was able to do this because he was not really concerned about being re-elected. He gladly announced his retirement from the Senate after two full terms at the age of 49. Could he have achieved more? Perhaps he could have. He told me that early in his Senate career he had a meeting with top national Republican leaders and financial contributors. They advised him that he could achieve about anything he wanted nationally and all he would have to change was his "world view." He never could do that. I believe he would argue today that our military, economic and political presence in nearly every country of the world and our intervention in the affairs of other nations, most recently in the Far East and the Middle East, have not made America or the world a safer place.

He believed strongly that our constitutional form of government would serve as a beacon of freedom that could be copied by other nations. However, he felt that it should never be forced on other sovereign nations.

He deeply loved his country. He once told me that if he had been right, he had not hurt his country, because others would take up the cause. If he had been wrong, he also had not hurt his country, because "there were too damned few of us to stop the liberal trend."

The rather unsympathetic Jenner biographer Michael Poder summarized Jenner's career as a public servant by saying he warned against the increased power of the presidency, the threat of an unresponsive bureaucracy, the futility of foreign aid, increasing national debt and the danger of international over commitment. Poder was correct: these were the central directions of the senator's political service and life. The question remains: was Bill Jenner the last of the isolationists fighting a rearguard action or was he simply ahead of his time?

Dad and Homer Capehart: two old veterans at the Republican National Convention, 1960

Barry Goldwater came to Indiana University in 1962 and posed with Dad and other Republican notables. I'm far left, then IU Republican Chairman Terry M. Grimm; Goldwater, State Treasurer Robert Hughes, Dad and Tom Huston, national chairman of Young Americans for Freedom.

Friendly rivals Bill Jenner and Governor Henry Schricker of Knox.

Dad loved his hunting dogs Sam and Ace. "These dogs will hunt!" Dad was an outdoorsman throughout his life.

Dad and Mom with Scott, Andy and Pat the day Anne and I were married. Bill Jenner became an instant grandfather as I wed the beautiful mother of these boys. Later Joe was born.

Dad and Mom were never happier than when at home in Bedford.

My wife Anne with Vice-President Dan Quayle (l) and Madison Courier *publisher Don Wallis.*

Wilma (third from left) was Dad's "second-in-command" and respected by all. Here she is in Chicago with Joe and Mom and on the right, Andy.

WORKS CONSULTED

Blake, George. *Paul V. McNutt: Portrait of a Hoosier Statesman*. Indianapolis: Central Publishing Co., 1966.

Cherny, Andrei. *The Candy Bombers: The Untold Story of the Berlin Airlift and America's Finest Hour*. New York: G. P. Putnam's Sons, 2008.

Gentry, Curt. *J. Edgar Hoover: The Man and the Secrets*. New York: W. W. Norton, 1991.

Gugin, Linda, and James E. St. Clair, eds. *The Governors of Indiana*. Indianapolis: Indiana Historical Society Press, 2006.

Herman, Arthur. *Joseph McCarthy: Re-examining the Life and Legacy of America's Most Hated Senator*. New York: The Free Press, 2000.

Jenner, William Ezra. Senator William Ezra Jenner political papers, 1931–1985, Hanover College Library Archives, Hanover, Indiana.

Jones, H. O. "Whitey." *A Twentieth Century History of Crawford County*. Chelsea, MI: Bookcrafters, 1984.

Laskey, Victor. *JFK: The Man and the Myth*. New York: Macmillan, 1963.

Leibowitz, Irving. *My Indiana*. Englewood Cliffs, NJ: Prentice-Hall, 1964.

Madison, James H. *Indiana Through Tradition and Change, 1920-1945*. Indianapolis: Indiana Historical Society, 1982.

Madison, James H. *The Indiana Way: A State History*. Bloomington and Indianapolis: Indiana University Press and Indiana Historical Society Press, 1986.

Morris, Robert. *No Wonder We Are Losing*. New York: The Book Binder, 1958.

Munger, Frank. *The Struggle for Republican Leadership in Indiana*. New York: McGraw-Hill, 1960.

Novak, Robert D. *The Prince of Darkness: 50 Years Reporting in Washington*. New York: Crown Forum, 2007.

Pickett, William B. *Homer E. Capehart: A Senator's Life, 1897–1979*. Indianapolis: Indiana Historical Society Press, 1990.

Pleasant, H. H. *Crawford County History 1818–1926*. Glenview, CA: Arthur H. Clark Co., 1926.

Poder, Michael. "The Senatorial Career of William E. Jenner." University of Notre Dame, PhD thesis, 1976.

Romerstein, Herbert and Breindel, Eric. *The Verona Secrets: Exposing Soviet Espionage and America's Traitors*. Washington, DC: Regnery Publishing, 2000.

Ross, Rodney. "Senator William E. Jenner: A Study of Coldwar Isolationism." Pennsylvania State University, EdD thesis, 1973.

Scheele, Raymond H. "Opportunity Structures and Factional Control:

The Case of Indiana in the 1930s and 1940s." Paper prepared for delivery at the Political Science Association Annual Meeting, Las Vegas, Nevada, March 8, 2007.

Schlesinger, Arthur M. Jr. *Robert Kennedy and His Times*. Boston: Houghton Mifflin, 1978.

Toland, John. *Infamy: Pearl Harbor and Its Aftermath*. Garden City, NY: Doubleday, 1982.

Tudor, David. Unpublished Interviews with Wm. E. Jenner, May 19, 1970.

Tudor, David. Interviews with political leaders regarding William E. Jenner, located at the Indiana University Center for the Study of History and Memory, Bloomington Indiana, Ashton-Aley West 264, Bloomington, IN.

Index

Roosevelt, President Franklin D. 9, 13, 15, 16, 18, 21, 38, 53-55, 77, 80, 112

S

T

U

V

W

X

Y

Z

About the author. . .

Bill Jenner has practiced law in Madison for 46 years. His law firm consists of six attorneys, including son Joe Jenner and ten staff persons. He says, "We have been a Martindale Hubbell A-rated firm for over 35 years."

He still goes when he can to the rustic cabin his family has enjoyed since the 1930s and enjoys his family and politics, even after all these years of living in the political arena.